COME AWAY MY LOVE

PURSUING INTIMACY THROUGH PRAYER

"My Lover is looking through the windows,
He is peering through the lattice.
He lifts up His voice and says to me,
"Arise, my love, my dove, my beautiful one,
and come away with me."

Song of Songs 2:9-10

By Cliff Baker

Cover design by Jon McCallum

Edited by Amy Lindholm

ISBN 978-0-578-05709-5

Printed in the United States of America

Published by Mighty In Spirit Ministries

Dedication

This book is dedicated to Nancy,
my wonderful wife, best friend
and greatest encourager.
Without her support and encouragement,
this book would not exist.

Thank you for believing in me.

Contents

Forward

It has been said that God comforts the afflicted and afflicts the comfortable. In reading this book you will find yourself wonderfully comforted by Cliff's journey. You will relate to how he goes through what you go through. It's like a wonderful, fragrant oil! You may find yourself greatly comforted saying, "I'm not crazy! I'm not the only one! I'm not the only Christian who can't get into this 'duty' called prayer. I know it's my responsibility but at least I know there are others who have difficulty praying." However God won't leave us there and neither does Cliff. You will enter a modern day contemplative journey where it's not just "grace grace" when it comes to your lack in prayer, but an uncomfortable prodding to not stay "stuck in prayerlessness". You will feel that you must get up, dust off, and go forward with a new hope and determination to tackle your part of covering the distance between you and God. We are all invited to enter into the watch of the Lord! Mark 13:37.

I enjoy writers who can make the profound things simple and the simple things profound. Cliff takes us through that simple little journey with profound results. So dive in! Why should we wait for another good conference when we have access to the very councils of God the Creator of all things? I say we go forward, walking with Cliff through his journey and seeking more and more of that friendship with God! We have the great privilege of encountering God every day. We don't have to wait for the next storm or lightning strike from heaven or the next anointed meeting to encounter Him. God is not far off but very near. Let's walk through that thin veil between the natural and supernatural and become a friend to the King of Glory. Let's not neglect this privilege of standing before the Creator of the universe and enjoying a conversation with Him. We all with unveiled faces can behold and enjoy Him!

Kirk Bennett
V.P. IHOPKC / Justice Division

Acknowledgments

A special thank you to four friends: Greg Hardman, Todd Faulkner, Rick Padgett, and Kelly Hahn. Your friendship, conversations, and encouragement have prompted me to complete this project. Thank you for your support and passionate hunger to know and love God.

To Amy Lindholm, an incredible editor and friend; thank you for the endless hours of proof reading, your insights, and suggestions. You have a way of challenging me to reach for my best. Thank you for helping me complete this project–you are amazing!

To my amazing wife, whose sharp eye and red pen helped with the final editing of this book. Thank you.

Introduction

An insatiable hunger gnaws at me every day. It never seems to go away. This hunger demands my attention even when I try to ignore it. What do I hunger for? Love. Yes! I confess my longing to be loved unconditionally, fervently, and eternally. I yearn for someone to go to great lengths just to be with me, someone who believes in me and smiles at the mention of my name. I know I am not alone in this quest for love. Countless stories have been told throughout history about mankind's search for this great love. Some people look to a mate for fulfillment, others to a life passion or cause to experience it. We all search for it in different ways. Ironically, as we search for love, the author of love, God Himself, waits patiently to reveal His love to our hearts! The God of the Universe went to inconceivable lengths to be with us and show us His love. He unveiled His love in the person of Jesus. The account of Jesus' life is the story of God's passionate pursuit for our hearts.

This book is about my heart's journey to grow deeper in intimacy with Jesus Christ. Once God's matchless love is experienced, an intense hunger for more will continue to increase. So, in part, I write out of a longing to encounter a deeper realm of His love, but also out of a desire to help others experience more of His love.

The moment I became a Christian, the desire for an intimate relationship with the Lord stirred within me. Even though I longed for love, I was unaware of what true intimacy looked like and unsure how to pursue it or cultivate it. Fortunately, Jesus showed me how. He began to reveal to me what I needed to know to embark on this journey. Jesus, through His word and the power of the Holy Spirit, can teach each one of us how to draw close to Him. His intense desire for a deeper relationship with us is greater than our weakness. His faithfulness exceeds our unfaithfulness and the Holy Spirit is eager to instruct us in the ways of love.

We are invited to participate in an amazing adventure with the Lord Jesus Christ. This adventure has surprises at every turn because God's ways are drastically different than ours and He loves more deeply than we love. His strategy for a closer relationship with us appears foreign at first. Yet, as we become acquainted with His ways, He will challenge us to move out of our comfort zones and into fresh new experiences with Him. As we allow Him to lead us into new territory, the inner secrets of His heart will be revealed to our hearts. Through the prophet Hosea the Lord declared: "Therefore I am now going to allure her; I will lead her into the desert and speak tenderly to her." (Hos 3:14)

Thankfully, God is relentless in His pursuit of an intimate relationship with us. Though we may reject His love, He runs after us. Our resistance is not an insurmountable obstacle to Him. He is driven by His own loving nature to beckon us closer to Him. Every day becomes a possibility for another encounter with His love.

Discovering God's heart is an amazing journey. Prayer plays an essential role in this journey. Through prayer, our Lord transforms our relationship with Him from a shallow acquaintance to an intimate friendship. As we grow in our knowledge of Him, we will mature in our faith and in our capacity to love others. We will discover an ability to do things we once imagined impossible.

During the learning process of understanding and experiencing God's heart, our perception of who we are and how we relate to Him changes. One discovery we will make is that prayer serves a far greater purpose than fulfilling daily petitions. Prayer is truly the catalyst by which we grow in intimacy with the Creator of the Universe. Of course we can ask God to meet our needs, but He has something far richer in store for us: a true relationship with Him.

The manner in which we relate to God composes the dynamic of prayer. How do we begin? God's word answers this question by instructing us that Christ is "to have first place in everything". (Col 1:18 NAS) In Mark 12:30, we are invited "to love the Lord our God with all our heart and with all our soul and with all our mind and with all our strength." As we take steps to love God with our entire being, He will begin to occupy the chief place in our lives and prayers. Prayer is the dwelling place where we can experience the dynamic exchange of love. God's outrageous love for us will be discovered during these times of intimate conversation and, to our surprise, we discover an ability to love Him back with a passion we never dreamed possible. Prayer becomes a celebration of our Father's love coupled with the living reality that Jesus Christ reigns in our hearts and lives.

Loving God is a process in which Christ first awakens our hearts to His affectionate, unconditional love. As we accept and embrace the Father's love, it frees us to love Him back with the same love in which He has loved us. Our love is expressed to Him as we abide in prayer and worship, listening to Him. As you read this book, my hope is to stir within you an insatiable hunger to begin this glorious journey of intimacy with your loving Father. Let the journey begin!

Chapter One

A Journey Into Intimacy

"The discussion of prayer is so great that it requires the Father to reveal it, his firstborn Word to teach it, and the Spirit to enable us to think and speak rightly of so great a subject."

Origen – Early Church theologian

It was a grey overcast autumn evening in the city of Portland. I had just finished leading a prayer meeting downtown with my friend David. After putting his musical equipment in his car, David approached me jingling a handful of loose change and smiling broadly. "I found this change on the sidewalk. It's prophetic!" he exclaimed.

David often surprised and enlightened me with his spiritual insights. But this was a little unusual, even for him. "Loose change–prophetic?" I replied, barely masking the sarcasm in my voice. Nonetheless curious, I held out my hand to see the coins–a nickel, a penny, a quarter, and two dimes. They looked pretty ordinary to me.

Ignoring my sarcasm, he went on, "You received a hand full of change and in it there is a pair of dimes; you are going to receive a major change in your *par-a-digm* concerning prayer."

"Great pun," I laughed, "But what makes you sure this is prophetic?"

David apparently felt no need to defend his proclamation. He smiled, looked me in the eye, and spoke calmly. "It is for you because you took the loose change."

As I drove home, I reflected on what he said. It was an odd way for God to tell me that things were going to shift. But it wasn't the first time God used an unconventional way to communicate. Why would God want to change the way I thought about prayer? As far as I knew, I had already gone through several major revisions in my concept and practice of prayer. I was seasoned. I could imagine subtle modifications but not a seismic shift. Little did I know, that was just what God had in mind. Over the next seven years, my life would be turned upside down and I would undergo a radical transformation in my understanding not only of prayer but of God Himself. The "pair of dimes:" paradigm shift would in essence move my prayers from a place of approaching God at a respectful distance to one in which I sat at His feet. This journey would be painful; the vast network of protective barriers I had erected over time would have to come down. The misconceptions I held about myself and God would have to be relinquished; and the sources of security which had served me so well–my ministry, my career, my teaching, would have to be released to

God in order that I might know Him and be known by Him. I am happy to tell you that the reward has been "a pearl of great price". I have learned to pray to God from a place of an intimate relationship.

After giving my life to Jesus, I have always set aside time for devotions. Early in the morning before work, I would usually spend an hour or more reading and studying the bible. I loved studying the word of God. I took notes and put them in notebooks. I wrote Scriptures down on 3x5 cards and worked on memorizing them. While reading the Bible was easy and enjoyable, praying was not. On a good day, I might talk to God for fifteen minutes. Usually I averaged about ten minutes. I had a narrow and limited perspective of prayer. Prayer was basically asking God to meet my needs and the needs of others. This perspective became my default setting for prayer.

Several years later, I began to feel a tug on my heart by the Lord to pray more. There was very little encouragement to pray in my circle of fellowship. In those days, I seldom heard a sermon on prayer. Most of my Christian friends never talked about their prayer life. We talked about many things in the bible but prayer was not usually one of them. Bringing up prayer seemed to make people feel uncomfortable. To avoid those awkward moments, we avoided the subject all together.

Due to my narrow concept of prayer, I interpreted God's request to pray more as a directive to collect more petitions and requests. So I began to gather prayer requests from other people. I wrote them down in my prayer journal and put a mark beside them if they were answered. My list began to grow, but the answers to my prayers didn't. I felt I was praying more and enjoying it less. I began to grow even more discouraged about prayer. The prayers that were answered seem to be fulfilled in the natural course of life. For example, if I prayed for people to be healed from the flu, they generally got well in three or four days. This did not seem like a major intervention by God. Wouldn't they normally have gotten well anyway? I was grateful to God for healing someone, but I wasn't sure it was the result of my prayers. I wanted concrete, tangible answers to prayer. I wanted to know if my prayers really made a difference. If they didn't, then why pray?

I struggled with the question, why even pray? If God already knew my needs, why should I have to tell Him? God was going to do what He wanted to do anyway, so why ask? Of course, I couldn't ignore the fact that the bible is filled with examples of people praying and communicating with God. It also seemed reasonable that Jesus wouldn't tell us to pray if it were a total waste of time, but I was confused about the purpose of prayer. It wasn't until years later that I realized my understanding about who God was and how He loves needed to be expanded in order to comprehend the purpose of prayer.

Another idea I wrestled with concerning prayer was repetition. I felt if I repeated a request several times then it was a prayer of unbelief. God heard me the first time. If He didn't answer me the first time, why should I believe He would answer me the second time? I didn't believe repetitive prayers would convince God to change His mind. Because of my narrow view of prayer I was ignorant of its primary purpose. I thought God was in the business of answering petitions; I didn't think He really wanted fellowship with me. The phrase "a personal relationship with God" appeared to merely be a sales tactic perpetuated by the Church. It was difficult for me to comprehend how reading a chapter a day, praying my petitions, and respecting the Lord out of fear would result in a personal relationship. At this point in my walk with the Lord, I lacked clarity regarding the dynamic of freedom granted to each of us by God which allows us to relate to Him in love.

I would never have admitted it at the time—because it would not sound spiritual—but praying was hard and at times even boring. I was having a crisis concerning prayer. The Holy Spirit was prompting me to pray more, yet at the same time I found prayer discouragingly hard and boring.

To help me find answers to my questions, I began to read books on the subject of prayer. As I dug deeper, I discovered there was a lot more to prayer than just petitions. While studying the Lord's Prayer in depth, I discovered that prayer contained many dimensions. I found six important elements in the Lord's Prayer: Worship, Intercession, Petition, Forgiveness, Spiritual Warfare, and Thanksgiving.

I quickly began to put these elements into practice. As a result, I started to enjoy prayer again. My prayer life expanded. The time I actually spent in prayer steadily grew. I found the more I read on prayer the more I prayed. The less I read on prayer, the less I prayed. Therefore, I began to read more books on prayer to motivate myself to pray.

Several years later I once again felt a tug on my heart by the Holy Spirit to pray even more. At the same time I began to grow discouraged with prayer. The questions I wrestled with in my heart were, "Why can't I pray fervently and faithfully by being motivated from the inside? Why do I need books on prayer to motivate me?" Besides, I was running out of good books on prayer to read. The books started sounding all the same. I kept sensing I was missing something in my prayer time. I felt there was more, but more of what? Were there more elements to add to my prayers?

As I mulled over these questions an idea came to me. It was a new direction for prayer; I would pray about prayer. Even with this new revelation, my old default setting regarding prayer kept popping up. Somehow, I still held onto the belief that I should tell God my needs and not worry about the relational aspect of prayer. How could I erase that setting and program a new one in its place? Old habits are hard to break!

When I began to seek the Lord about how to pray, He answered me in unexpected ways. One day the Lord impressed on my heart to spend time alone with Him from 6:00 am to 7:00 am on Tuesday mornings at the church building. Nobody was there. I didn't have to worry about disturbing anyone. During that time of prayer I strongly felt His presence. I began to pray in ways I had never experienced before. I spoke out loud to the Lord as if we were having a conversation. Instead of sitting to pray, I began walking around while praying and reading the Scriptures aloud. This brought a whole new level of energy and freshness to my prayer time. I began to worship the Lord more and more by playing worship music. It was encouraging to worship and pray at the same time. As I realized that prayer and worship were different ways to express my heart to God, I discovered I could sing prayers and pray songs. I began to consistently feel the presence of God and enjoy the time I spent with Him.

This continued for several months until one Tuesday morning I didn't feel His presence nor could I pray. During the first ten minutes, I tried every conceivable type of prayer I knew, but they all failed to give me that same sense of His presence. Out of discouragement I decided to go downstairs to work. As soon as I touched the doorknob, the Holy Spirit asked, "Did I not ask for one hour?" Under conviction, I went back to the middle of the room and tried to pray out loud once more. My prayers did not even make it to the ceiling. By this time it was 6:15 a.m. I felt I was wasting time, so I decided once again to start my day in the church office. As soon as I touched the doorknob, the Holy Spirit for a second time spoke to my heart, "Did I not ask for one hour?" I went back to my seat and sat down. In silence, I sat for the next forty five minutes. When the hour was up, I went downstairs to work. On the way I asked the Lord, "What are you after?" No answer came.

For the next several weeks the Tuesday morning prayer time was wonderful again. Then one morning it happened again. I didn't feel His presence nor could I pray. This time I knew that leaving the room was not an option. I was going to give God the full hour no matter what. After about twenty minutes of silence, my mind began to wander as I looked out the window and thought to myself, "This is boring!" As soon as that thought entered my mind, the Lord spoke, "It is not boring for me to hang out with you." I was broken and began to weep, "Lord I don't understand what you want. What are you after?" I had a hard time imagining that the Lord of creation wanted to "hang out" with me. It seemed utterly inconceivable to me that God would enjoy being with me. To my surprise, I had no concept of "being" with Jesus. How could Jesus want me to sit in silence with Him for the sole reason of enjoying each other's company? Why would God want to spend time with me? With all my weaknesses and struggles, I believed I was a huge disappointment to God.

Intellectually I knew that Jesus died for me and that eternal life was to know Jesus and the Father in a personal way, but it had truly never registered in my heart that the Father really liked me and wanted to be with me. I perceived myself to be a mere sinner saved by grace. I felt the Lord tolerated me and had to put up with my weaknesses. It concerned me that God might be growing weary of the cycle of failures that seemed to plague my life. I became accustomed to going to God with my requests, asking for forgiveness, thanking Him for His provision, and surrendering my will to Him. When I was finished, I didn't linger. I left.

The idea of "being" with God took some getting used to since the old pattern of our relationship was all I knew. I did not realize at first what God was doing. It did not occur to me that God wanted to give Himself to me in a real and tangible way so that I could experience peace, rest and most of all, His love. The God I knew was far away, not close at hand. Prayer was more like a long distance phone call rather than a conversation with someone in the same room. I honored God and worshiped Him from a distance. He was to me a benevolent King and Lord. His Lordship was the central focus of my worship. The word "Lord" meant to me "boss." God was the boss of my life.

As my boss, I obeyed Him out of respect and fear. I wanted to be a good employee in His kingdom, yet I was not accustomed to having an intimate close relationship with any earthly boss. Prayer was a matter of doing business with God and then going about my day. I even applied this sense of distance to reading the Bible. While I loved studying God's word, it was more like an interesting but antiquated, historical document rather than a love letter meant to speak to my heart.

During the months in which I spent time alone with God on Tuesday mornings, He awakened a desire in me for a deeper relationship with Him. He created a hunger and thirst within my heart for more of His love. I had a longing in my heart for God that I had never experienced before. At last God was answering my prayer about prayer: He was creating an inner motive in my heart to seek Him. My heart was awakened to

His love. This marked the beginning of a new dimension in my journey of prayer. Prayer began to be about an intimate relationship with the almighty God.

As I realized I could have a closer relationship with God, I became intensely curious about His love. I kept asking Him to show me His love and to show me the places where I could find more of His love. The Shulammite in the Song of Songs asked the same question; "Tell me, O you whom my heart loves, where do you feed your flock, where do you make it rest at noon? Why should I be like a veiled woman beside the flocks of your friends?" (S.O.S. 1:7) Her heart was awakened by the love of God and she wanted more. She wanted to be fed by the Lord Himself and to rest in His love. She no longer wanted to be a distant "veiled" admirer of Him, but rather an intimate lover. Many of us are like the Shulammite, not knowing where to go to feed on His love.

The Lord has an answer for us in His words to the Shulammite; "If you do not know, most beautiful of women, follow the tracks of the sheep and feed your little goats beside the shepherds' tents." (S.O.S. 1:8) The Shulammite was expecting the Lord Himself to teach her, but the Lord tells her instead to follow in the steps of those who had gone before her and learn from them. Throughout the centuries, there have been many lovers of God whose lives laid a path we can follow in our journey of intimacy with Him. We can learn from them how to sit at the feet of Jesus and receive His love as Mary of Bethany and others did.

Before long, I came to love prayer because it began to feel like I was spending time with the lover of my soul. Prayer became a delight. My love for God was growing as well. Then, the unpredictable happened. One day while praying, I felt the Lord say, "I want you to go and pray eight hours every day for six months." Words from the Song of Songs were imprinted on my heart: "Arise, my love, my dove, my beautiful one, and come away with me. Look, winter is past, the rains are over and gone." (S.O.S. 2:10) From this verse Jesus spoke to me, "You have been asking for My presence so come away with me. Come, enter into a new season with Me, a season of ministering to Me." "O my dove, in the clefts of the rock, in the secret places of the rock, let me see your face, let me hear your voice, for your voice is sweet, and your face is lovely." (S.O.S. 2:14)

I froze in fear. Rather than feeling delight at this invitation, I felt panic. My first thoughts were, "How will I survive? I will have to quit my job as an associate pastor to do what He is asking. How will I finance this time of prayer?" I had never heard of anyone financing another person's desire to go pray seven days a week. My next thought was; "What if I fail?" In short, I was scared. The Lord was asking me to come away with Him. He was asking me to come to where He was, but He was outside my boat walking on the water. To go where He was, I would have to step out of my comfort zone. It didn't look safe. Not only that, I had no paradigm for such a calling. During all my years of ministry, I was not aware of any other person God had called to pray all day long. I thought God called individuals to minister to people. This call to prayer did not fit into my evangelical charismatic doctrine. Could God really be asking me to leave all that was familiar—ministering to people—so that I could primarily minister to Him? Would God, who is love, ask me to do something that didn't appear to be safe?

Fear was drowning out the voice of God. Fear magnifies the desire to be secure and safe. Fear can masquerade itself as the voice of reason, good sense and respectability. Fear makes the pursuit of earthly security seem like the most reasonable choice. How can you argue against caution? What defense can you muster against the desire to be safe?

I assured myself that it was entirely reasonable to ask for a well marked map, or at least a G.P.S. Wasn't it generally considered responsible and prudent to seek out provision and insurance when embarking on an adventure? To venture out into uncharted territory without these provisions seemed foolish. But the voice of eternity asked something different of me: to trust and believe.

In the C.S. Lewis classic "The Lion, The Witch, and The Wardrobe," Lucy asks Mr. and Mrs. Beaver about Aslan the Lion. "Is he quite safe? I shall feel rather nervous about meeting a lion." The child is told by Mrs. Beaver, "That you will, dearie, and no mistake. If there's anyone who can appear before Aslan without their knees knocking, they're either braver than most or just plain silly." Still, Lucy isn't convinced. "Then he isn't safe?" she asks. "Safe?" said Mr. Beaver "don't you hear what Mrs. Beaver tells you? Who said anything about safe?' Course he isn't safe. But he's good. He's the king, I tell you."

God does not appear safe because He is not predictable in His actions. We do not know what He may ask us to do. Did He not ask Jonah to preach to his fierce enemies and Hosea to marry a prostitute? Have you noticed He rarely calls us to convenience but rather to inconvenience? He never seems to call us to the possible but to the impossible. On the other hand, He can always be trusted because He never changes. He cannot deny who He is. He is always Holy Love.

In the parable of the talents, Jesus taught that "playing it safe" was the worse choice anyone could make. When the master in the story discovers that the servant to whom he had given one talent had buried it, he responded: "That's a terrible way to live! It's criminal to live cautiously like that! If you knew I was after the best, why did you do less than the least? The least you could have done would have been to invest the sum with the bankers, where at least I would have gotten a little interest." The master vents his anger even further by proclaiming a woeful fate for the servant. "Take the thousand and give it to the one who risked the most," he states. "And get rid of this "play-it-safe" who won't go out on a limb. Throw him out into utter darkness." (Matt 25:28-30 MSG) What is this? It's criminal to live cautiously? Reading this parable at a time when God was calling me out on a limb made me realize I had been living cautiously all my life. Now, He was asking me to step out of the familiar into the unfamiliar, from the explainable to the unexplainable, from the predictable to the unpredictable.

Was I willing to follow Him into the unknown? That was the question I wrestled over for the next six months. I repeatedly asked the Lord about my concerns for finances and for the future. He never answered those prayers; instead He asked me, "What are you going to do with that word?" I finally surrendered to His word and said yes. That very act of obedience was followed by a flood of amazing peace which is impossible to describe. Once I obeyed, the Lord confirmed in many ways that this was His plan for me.

One week after making the decision to obey the Lord, I began to struggle with the consequences of that decision. In order to make the transition as smooth as possible for the church, I decided to take three months to shift my pastoral responsibilities over to others. It was during this period of transition that the reality of my decision sunk in and it became overwhelming. I felt that my ministry was over and I was now entering into obscurity. Would I ever get my ministry back? I wondered. The fears began to slowly seep in again. What followed was this wonderful dialogue with God.

The Lord spoke: "My son, until now you have lived a common life, not much different than most people. I am calling you to something more. I am calling you to a deeper walk with Me. Because of the love in My heart, which I have had for you from the time of your creation, I am not going to leave you alone. I am drawing you away to Myself with the cords of everlasting love. I gave you a new heart when you were born again. Through the revelation of My love, I am awakening a stronger desire in this new heart of yours to be more closely united to Me. As a result you will no longer be content to live at a distance from Me. Listen carefully; I am not asking for your help, I am asking for you. I am asking for the devotion of your heart. I did not call you to work for Me, but to be with Me. Pay very close attention to My call upon your life. What I am asking of you in this new adventure with Me is a whole new way of life. It's a life that reflects My life. It's a life that is dependent upon Me for life. You have not lived this way before. Not to this degree. Do not lean on your own understanding. For you do not understand what I am going to do. It's by My grace that you will be able to walk in this new way of life that you are deliberately choosing. I am delighted that you said yes. I am eagerly waiting for the time we will spend together."

I replied to the Lord in prayer, saying, "Lord Jesus, bind me to You with the cords of love! I do not want to live at a distance from You. I want to be with You. I am excited about drawing closer to You in intimacy and learning the ways of Your heart. I desire to walk with You in a deeper way. But Lord Jesus, there are moments in the day that fear attacks my heart. At times I am flooded with fear, wondering if I will be able to make it and resist the enemy's subtle temptations. Will I be able to carry out Your assignment on my life? You asked me to pray eight hours a day; I don't know if I can do it." Fear choked my heart. I was inundated with questions that had no answers. "Are you crazy for stepping down from your job to pursue this new adventure? What about your responsibilities in life? What about your family? Do you really think the Lord is going to supply your needs?" I searched for words to respond. I told the Lord: "God, I am afraid I may fail You and disappoint or embarrass You."

The Lord spoke to my heart again, saying, "My son, I did not give you a spirit of fear, but a spirit of power, of love and of self discipline. The Holy Spirit I gave you, that abides within you, will help you conquer your fears. Yield to Him, keep your attention focused on Me! My love for you is measured by the depth of My sacrifice in freeing you for Myself. I am a jealous God. I will not let you go. As you grow in understanding the depth of My love, it will conquer your fears. Cultivate My love. You will not embarrass Me, for I am not ashamed to call you brother. Now is the time for you to look forward and forget what is behind you. It is a new day arising. Do not focus on what you already have attained, but on where you are going and what you still need."

Despite God's encouragement, I continued to wrestle with fear. Several weeks later I was deeply anxious about how I would sustain such a vigorous prayer schedule for six months. I wondered if I could ask other people to come and pray with me at different times during the day. Their presence would encourage me to keep praying. I also asked the Lord to give me grace to fast for the first forty days. If I fasted, I knew it would help move my mind and heart into prayer. Several days later, the Lord answered my prayer. "I will give you grace to fast for forty days, but you cannot pray with others during the first forty days of this journey. I want you to spend this time alone with Me."

Alone! Why did I need to be alone? I had no grid for being alone for forty days of prayer. I couldn't comprehend why He was not allowing me to pray with people. Finally, I realized that He was cutting away my unhealthy dependence on people in order to learn to lean on Him. He was trying to show me that only He could sustain me. He is the God of all comfort and He wants me to depend upon Him and run to Him first, not to people.

The Lord wonderfully provided a place for me to pray. I was given access to a building twenty four hours a day for the entire six months. Thus, began my new journey of prayer. I went to prayer while others went to work. Each day as I began to pray, I strongly felt His presence. Slowly I began to build endurance in the different expressions of prayer. I would pray one way for an hour or two before changing to another expression. For example, I would pray in the Spirit for one or two hours then pray meditatively on the Scripture for several more hours. After taking a break, I would begin again with worship, and then move into silent prayer. Each day my routine of prayer would change. Some days were challenging, but over all I enjoyed going to God in prayer.

During the six months of prayer, the Lord began to reveal

more of His love to me in interesting ways. He challenged me regarding my ambitions and motivations for ministry. He exposed insecurities and weaknesses I had concealed through pride. He revealed to me my desire for the approval of man and convicted me regarding my insensitivity towards some of my friends in ministry. But even as He showed me these flaws and convicted me of my sins, I felt an outpouring of His love and acceptance.

His love became more of a wonderful mystery to me. My encounters with His love left me bewildered. When I looked into the eyes of the One who is love, I quickly discovered that my love was inadequate. It was frightening to be in the presence of perfect love which is selfless and sacrificial since I was filled with selfishness and self preservation. When I chose to gaze at the One who out of love gave His life for me, I realized that I was looking into my own destiny. I too would have to learn to give sacrificially. Perhaps the most important thing God taught me concerned my concept of who I was and how I could relate to Him. For my sake, He wanted me to relate to Him as my Father, putting Him in the center of my life so I could realize the sonship to which I had been called.

As I meditated on the revelation of His love, it became an even deeper mystery to me. The more insight I received into the nature and character of His love, the more I became astonished with the awesomeness of love's exquisite beauty. As He unfolded the multiple aspects of His love to my heart, my mind was thrown into a tailspin. I had no frame of reference to categorize what He was revealing to me. When I tried to rationalize His love it didn't seem rational or logical. Instead, God's love was indeed that which "no eye has seen, nor ear heard, nor the human heart conceived," (1 Cor 2:9) for God has revealed it to us by His Spirit. When my heart was touched by His love, my mind seemed to be blinded by the light of His love. It was like walking out of a dimly lit building into the blazing noonday sun. At first, the bright light can be blinding but then after awhile your eyes gradually adjust to its intensity. Once my eyes adjusted to the brilliant light of love, things changed.

It was necessary to re-think my relationship with the Lord. I could no longer relate to Him as I had in the past. The words I had once used to define my life with God ceased to reflect what He was doing in my heart. My default setting for prayer and the way I related to God needed to change. The working paradigm I once had concerning prayer was now inadequate.

As I searched for a concept that could adequately describe the life as well as the heart of prayer, I discovered Mary of Bethany. She is mentioned three times in the gospels. In each occurrence, she is found in the same position: at the feet of Jesus. Mary "sat at the Lord's feet listening to what he said." (Luke 10:39) In John 11:32, she fell at Jesus' feet and poured out the sadness of her heart. The last recorded occurrence portrays Mary at Jesus' feet extravagantly worshipping Him. She poured expensive perfume on Jesus' feet and wiped them with her hair. (Jn 12:3) These scriptures show Mary of

Bethany growing and progressing in her love, freedom, and intense passion for the One that loved her.

To think of prayer in these displays of affection—sitting at Jesus' feet, listening to His words, pouring out my heart to Him, and worshipping Him extravagantly—was revolutionary to me. The phrase "sitting at Jesus' feet" is one of the best descriptions of prayer. When I began to embrace this image in prayer, it brought a whole new dimension to my paradigm of prayer. Instead of saying "I am going to pray" I began to say "I am going to sit at Jesus' feet." Instead of making a long distance phone call to God who is on the other side of the universe, I began to meet with my Beloved. Now when I pray, I realize that Jesus is with me right here, right now, fellowshipping with me.

As I meditated on what "sitting at Jesus' feet" might imply, several new ideas began to emerge that helped me redefine and reshape my concept of prayer. This opened the door for a deeper and more real relationship with the Lord in true intimacy.

A PRAYER FOR INTIMACY

Father, You drew me to Yourself with cords of love. Never in my wildest dreams would I have ever thought You would call me away to be with You in prayer. You call and then You give grace to respond to that call. You say, "Come! Just be with Me! Sit at My feet and learn from Me." Instead of joy, fear rose in my heart. It was like a roar of a lion that tried to drown out Your voice. Even though You asked me to do something that appeared frightening, there was love in Your voice that drew me to You. You saw my weakness. You saw my fears. You gave me grace to say yes.

The still small voice of Your love conquers the roar of the lion. Lord, as I "come away" to be close to You I ask that You give me a listening heart and a willing spirit to obey You in all that You reveal to me. Amen!

Chapter Two

Jesus' Longing For Fellowship

"The man-God's man-is made in the closet. His life and his profoundest convictions were born in his secret communion with God. The burdened and tearful agony of his spirit, his weightiest and sweetest messages were received when alone with God. Prayer makes the man." E.M. Bounds

Surprisingly, our greatest hindrance to intimacy with Christ is often our service for Him. One reason we lack a close relationship with God is that we think our highest calling is to serve Him rather than to know and love Him. We believe that from our service we will grow closer to God when in fact, it is just the opposite. Elevating ministry to the highest calling greatly distorts our relationship with God and reduces our prayers to being tools for ministry rather than a means of drawing close to God. The Scriptures are clear that our first priority as Christians is to pursue the Lord for the Lord's sake. From that place of intimacy, our true service to Christ arises. Loving the Lord our God with all our heart, soul, and mind must be the primary focus of our lives. (See Luke 10:27) If we don't know God well, we cannot possibly know what He wants us to do and how He wants us to do it. If God is not first in our lives, we will inevitably fall short of fulfilling Jesus' commandment to love one another as He loved us.

Several weeks into my six month prayer journey, the Lord began to dismantle my concept of ministry with a barrage of questions. T.S. Elliot once advised, "Oh my soul, be prepared to meet Him who knows how to ask questions." If only I had been prepared! The Lord knew just the right questions to ask. His questions are not designed to gather information but rather to expose what is in our hearts. The Lord asked me, "What qualifies you to minister?" This simple question unraveled me; it revealed my hidden fears, insecurities, and doubts. I felt as if I had been asked to defend my qualifications and present my credentials to a jury of my peers. I became a little uncomfortable and defensive. Thoughts raced through my mind. I had spent over twenty years in full time ministry! Am I qualified? What if I am not qualified to minister? Was all the ministry of the last twenty years mere hay, wood, and stubble? Doubts crept in: maybe I didn't attend the right college, take the right classes or get the right training. Maybe I hadn't kept up on the latest scholarly research. But then it hit me. This wasn't another colleague asking the question; this was the Holy Spirit. In the midst of this whirlwind of self doubt, the Holy Spirit spoke to my heart, saying, "These things do not qualify you to minister. You can learn a lot from these things and still not know Me.

What qualifies you to minister is spending time with Me." I was speechless. Spending time with the Lord qualifies me to minister? Is drawing close to God a prerequisite to service? I began to reflect on the ministry classes from the bible school I attended. Knowing God had definitely not been the main emphasis in my course of study. I loved the classes, learning a lot concerning biblical doctrine and scholarship. I was taught how to preach sermons and received wonderful information about effectively serving and ministering to people. But in truth, I had not learned how to grow in intimacy with the Lord. I came away with more knowledge *about* God without truly *knowing Him* .

We can know and even understand the teachings of the bible, but do we experience the reality of its message? Many of us have dedicated our lives and sacrificed much to serve God, but sadly have spent little time in actual pursuit of a relationship with God. As a consequence, few may have experienced the vibrant relationship with God that the scriptures promise. In asking us to preach the good news to others, the Lord did not call us to merely share information we've read in the Bible, but to be a witness to the reality of Christ in our lives.

If knowing God and spending time with Him qualifies us to minister, one might ask, "What is ministry?" On the surface we may think of things like preaching, teaching, helping the poor, counseling, and evangelism. But these acts of service, like biblical knowledge, are not ministry unless shaped and inspired by God's love. The Holy Spirit began to reveal to me a better definition of ministry. It is giving God to others: His love, His kindness, His peace. A tragic error occurs when we minister without giving out God's love.

This was a wake up call and a challenge. I asked myself, "Can I preach the Bible, feed the poor, counsel people and not give out Christ? Can I minister and not communicate Christ? Have I substituted events, programs, and activities for His presence? Have I replaced His presence with preaching about His presence?"

Paul emphasized that the fragrance of the knowledge of Christ should emanate from us. (See 2 Cor 2:14) How can we become conduits through which Christ's presence is released? I wondered. I knew how to study and present a message, but how could I obtain His presence? My knowledge about Christ had increased, but had I really grown to know Him?

Paul shared that he came to a place where he could say, "I no longer live, but Christ lives in me. The life I live in the body, I live by faith in the Son of God, who loved me and gave himself for me." (Gal 2:21) This scripture reveals that we are to personally know Christ in such an intimate way that we impart Him in all we do. How is this possible?

I discovered the answer by looking at the lives of those who spent time with Jesus. As flawed as they were as human beings, the disciples were nonetheless living breathing examples of people who were filled with the Spirit of Christ. In Acts, the Sanhedrin, the official rulers of Israel, said of Peter and John. "When they saw the courage of Peter and

John and realized that they were unschooled, ordinary men, they were astonished and they took note that these men had been with Jesus."(Acts 4:13) Do people say the same thing about us when we minister?

One of the greatest examples of a person being with Jesus comes from the story of Mary and Martha. "Jesus and his disciples were traveling through the village of Bethany when a woman named Martha opened her home to him." (Lk 10:38) The visit came after a tiring and arduous time of ministry in which Jesus had been rejected by the citizens of Korazin and Bethsaida who did not believe in Him or accept His miracles. (Lk 10:13) Weary and perhaps discouraged, Jesus and His disciples found welcome hospitality in the home of Martha and her sister Mary.

In the story we see that Mary chose to sit at Jesus' feet and listen to all He had to say. Martha, on the other hand, was distracted by all the preparations for the meal. Perhaps noticing that Mary was in a better place, Martha approached Jesus and asked Him, "Lord, don't you care that my sister has left me to do the work by myself? Tell her to help me!" Jesus replied: "Martha, Martha, you are worried and upset about many things, but only one thing is needed. Mary has chosen what is better, and it will not be taken away from her." (Lk 10:39-42)

For a long time, I was bewildered by the Lord's answer to Martha. After all, Martha had invited Jesus and His disciples to her home. She was in the kitchen diligently working to prepare lunch for her guest. Wasn't Mary shirking her responsibility by sitting at Jesus' feet leaving Martha to do all the work? Martha's request seemed so reasonable: there was work to be done, and two sets of hands are better than one. Why didn't Jesus just say, "Martha, I want to commend you for inviting me to your home and I honor you for all your hard work. Mary, get into the kitchen and help your sister."

The answer Jesus gave turned everything upside down for me. He did not commend Martha for her hard work and responsible nature. Instead, He lovingly rebuked her for worrying and getting upset about unimportant matters. He honored Mary for making the best choice. What this story so brilliantly illustrates is that Jesus' values and priorities are definitely different from ours.

Jesus was looking for fellowship and friendship. Out of love, He came to serve, to love and to be known. He desired that those whom He loved would respond back in love. Jesus did not die in order to have a bunch of hired servants who would relate to Him as a master. He sacrificially gave Himself for people who, out of love for Him, would choose to work alongside Him and relate to Him as the lover of their souls. Mary saw Isaiah 54:5 in Jesus. "Our Maker is our Husband." The One who fashioned us is the One who intensely desires to be in an intimate relationship with us. Hosea tells us, "In that day, "declares the Lord," you will call Me 'my husband', you will no longer call Me 'my master.'" (Hos 2:16) In these scriptures, the word "husband" speaks of the covenant love God wants to have with us. Mary saw the heart of Jesus. It was not the heart of a cruel taskmaster but the heart of a loving Bridegroom.

Martha and Mary represent two different choices. One choice appears unconventional but moves us nearer to the heart of God. The other appears to be good, but keeps us at a safe distance. Martha represents a way of serving Jesus which lacks relationship. If we want to know Him, really know Him, we have to choose to draw near the way Mary did in order to catch glimpses of His heart.

Another theme explored in the story of Mary and Martha is that of distraction. The story tells us that Martha "was distracted by all the preparations that had to be made." Interestingly, the word "preparations" is the same word for "ministry." The word basically means "to wait on tables." Martha was in fact distracted by her ministry. How ironic! Martha invites the Son of God into her home and her ministry to the Son of God becomes a distraction from the Son of God.

Martha was working for the Lord and as a result missed fellowshipping with the Lord. Martha in her ambition to work for the Lord ended up forfeiting her proximity to Him. His presence was supposed to be a delight but instead, became a burden. C.S. Lewis noted that "there have been some who were so occupied in spreading Christianity that they never gave a thought to Christ... It is the subtlest of all the snares."[1]

Martha, being distracted and worried, became frustrated and interrupted Jesus. Martha must have thought that Jesus would certainly take her side. It was obvious to her that Mary's place was in the kitchen helping out. In her mind, Jesus was overlooking this glaring injustice!

Isn't it interesting that the one who was working for God accused Him of lack of concern? Martha accused the One who cared the most. Peter tells us to "cast all your anxiety on Him because He cares for you." (1 Pet 5:7) Out of her frustration, Martha told the Son of God what to do. She was trying to persuade Jesus to help her fulfill her own agenda. How many of us have tried to micro-manage God through prayer? Have you ever tried to tell God what to do and at times even advise Him how to do it?

A peculiar phenomenon seems to occur when we work for Christ. When ministry supersedes all else in our lives and especially with any degree of success it causes us to be susceptible to distractions and worry. Instead of focusing on knowing Jesus' heart, we become overly attached to maintaining a successful ministry. Fear drives this worry. The fear of failure looms in the hearts of many hard-working ministers becoming the motivation for ministry. This effects decisions, prayers, and relationships. It causes people to work harder, but who is really being served? Ourselves or God? Working for Christ can blind us from seeing as He sees and keeps us from receiving the intent of His heart. If the fruit of our labor is distraction and anxiety, it should be obvious that we are out of step and have lost sight of what is important.

At times, we have all been motivated to work for compliments, recognition, and the approval of others. It's human nature. But ultimately, our service is to honor Jesus not ourselves. Initially, most of us begin ministry with the desire to glorify Christ, but often end up focusing on becoming successful in the eyes of man. A warning sign of this misdirected focus is to react like Martha, becoming upset when no one notices or appreciates our service. It's tragic to think we can work all our lives creating a beautiful meal for God only to discover He never ordered it.

Jesus tells Martha that Mary made the better choice by electing to be with Him. He points out that the experience of being with Him "will not be taken away from her." In other words, it has eternal value. While Martha desired to move the hand of God, Mary desired to know the heart of God. While Martha wanted Jesus to hear her and respond to her, Mary wanted to hear from Jesus and respond to Him. Martha, like so many of us, missed the fundamental reason why Jesus came to rescue us. He came to be known, not served. Jesus Himself said, "For even the Son of Man did not come to be served, but to serve, and to give His life as a ransom for many." (Mark 10:45) No matter how sincere Martha was in wanting to serve the Son of God, she missed the intent of Jesus' heart.

Contrary to popular belief, the supreme calling on our lives is not ministry. It is intimacy. Jesus is after followers who know and love Him as friends. Jesus said, "Now this is eternal life: that they may know you, the only true God, and Jesus Christ, whom you have sent." (John 17:3 NIV) Notice that Jesus did not say that eternal life is serving God, but knowing God. The word "know" here is referring to knowing in an intimate, experiential way.

The risen Christ had to correct the early church in their priorities and in their thinking. In the book of Revelation Jesus confronted the church in Ephesus. (See Rev. 2:1-7). He warned them that if they did not turn back to their first love He would remove their lamp stand. The lamp stand represents the Church. Why is the Lord's warning so severe? The Ephesian church was faithful to orthodoxy and hard work. Wasn't that enough? In the mist of diligently studying the word of God, rejecting heresy, and serving others, they forgot the most important thing: their first love. They lost sight of the fundamental reason Jesus had redeemed them, which was to be a living witness to the love of God. We are called to be the light of the world; that light is God's love shining through us as we live out a loving relationship with Him and express that love to others.

You can also see the desire of Jesus' heart when He spoke to the church in Laodicea "Here I am! I stand at the door and knock. If you hear my voice and open the door, I will come in and eat with you, and you will eat with me." (Rev 3:20 NCV) His expressed desire is to commune with us. This is the very reason He redeemed us.

The Apostle Paul warned the Corinthian church to keep their devotion to Christ pure. "But [now] I am fearful lest that even as the serpent beguiled Eve by his cunning, so your minds may be corrupted and seduced from wholehearted and sincere and pure devotion to Christ." (2 Cor. 11:3 AMP) How easy it is to shift from a pure devotion to Christ based on love and grace, to a performance-driven acceptance based on service. In

Roxanne Brandt's book "Ministering To The Lord," she reveals the misconception that we are saved in order to serve or repay God:

> "How wrong the Church has been to teach new Christians that we are saved to serve God. No! We are saved primarily because He wants us for Himself... God isn't in the business of saving people because He needs servants to win the world for Christ... Yet many Christians believe that they are working for a semi-impotent God who needs their help and expects them to repay Him. The Bible never once tells us to do anything for God. It tells us that in His love and grace, God chose to involve us in what He was doing. We can work with Him and allow Him to work through us."[2]

Paul tells the men of Athens that "the God who produced and formed the world and all things in it, being Lord of heaven and earth, does not dwell in handmade shrines. Neither is He served by human hands, as though He lacked anything, for it is He Himself Who gives life and breath and all things to all [people]." (Acts 17:24-25 AMP) The Father is not one who takes, but one who gives.

The scriptures make it abundantly clear that the Father is not the needy one; we are. He is not asking for our help, but offering His. The word describes God as acting "*on behalf of those who wait for him*" and "*helps those who remember his ways.*"(Isa. 64:4-5 Emphasis added). They portray God as one who is literally searching the earth "to strengthen those whose hearts are fully committed to him." (2 Chron. 16:9)

The author of Hebrews prayed that the Lord Jesus would "equip you with everything good for doing his will, and may he work in us what is pleasing to him." (Heb 13:20) The Lord gives us the ability to do His will. Jesus' kingdom is not sustained by our power, energy or efforts. Rather, we are strengthened and equipped by His power. Jesus Himself said, "For even the Son of Man did not come to be served, but to serve, and to give his life as a ransom for many." (Mark 10:45)

God is all-sufficient and complete. He does not depend on anything outside of Himself, and has no need. The great theologian A.W. Tozer put it this way:

> "Need is a creature-word and cannot be spoken of the Creator. God has a voluntary relation to anything He has made, but He has no necessary relation to anything outside of Himself. His interest in His creatures arises from His sovereign good pleasure, not from any need those creatures can supply nor from any completeness they can bring to Him who is complete in Himself."[3].

God is all-powerful and all-knowing. He does not need to be schooled since He knows everything. He does not need to be counseled because He is an all-wise God. Paul declares, "For who has known the mind of the Lord and who has understood His thoughts, or who has [ever] been His counselor? Or who has first given God anything that he might be paid back or that he could claim a recompense?" (Rom 11:34-35 AMP)

If the Father is all-knowing and all-wise, then how should we approach Him with our requests? Martha tried to tell Jesus what to do and how to do it. She received a loving rebuke, yet Mary, who sat at the feet of Jesus, is ascribed as having chosen the "one thing" that was better. If Jesus came to love and be loved, to be known through fellowship, perhaps seeking intimacy with Jesus is the wisest path to take. Waiting, listening, and quieting our hearts at Jesus' feet, to gain His perspective is not being idle as Martha may have thought. In fact, it may be the most important action we can practice in our walk with God.

Even though the Father doesn't *need* our love or our fellowship, the mysterious wonder is that He desires it. When Jesus came to Martha's house He was looking for more than food and shelter; He was looking for fellowship. Fellowship is the primary reason Incarnate Love came to earth. He came to reveal the heart of the Father to us. We really can't get to know God unless we spend time with Him. Spending time with Him is called prayer.

As we minister to others, we can only give away what we have. Knowledge about Jesus can only be given as information, but a real relationship with Him cultivates and gives away exactly what many are seeking: the love of God.

Without abiding in Christ, there is little we can do for others, try as we might. Who can perform miracles, such as healing the sick and raising the dead, without Christ? Can we love sacrificially like Christ or love our enemies without knowing Christ's love? Can we forgive seventy times a day, the person who offends us, without God's help? We cannot be dispensers of righteousness, peace, and joy without Christ for these things are of the Holy Spirit. (See Rom 14:17) In truth, we are not capable of offering anything of eternal value to mankind without abiding in Christ.

No program, event, or institutional degree can produce the life and power of God. Ministry, therefore, is the natural overflow of a vibrant, intimate relationship with Jesus. Many ministers have exhausted themselves serving God, growing frustrated and anxious. This is why Jesus said, "Are you tired? Worn out? Burned out on religion? Come to me. Get away with Me and you'll recover your life. I'll show you how to take a real rest. Walk with Me and work with Me — watch how I do it. Learn the unforced rhythms of grace. I won't lay anything heavy or ill-fitting on you. Keep company with me and you'll learn to live freely and lightly." (Matt 11:28-30 MSG)

It is important to learn how to be with Jesus and keep company with Him, finding rest in His presence. "For anyone who enters God's rest also rests from his own work, just as God did from His. Let us, therefore, make every effort to enter that rest..." (Heb 4:10) To "rest from our work" does not mean we stop working, but it does mean that we stop striving and acting out of our own anxiety and fear. Learning God's ways will help us enter into His rest. The writer of the book of Hebrews wrote, "their hearts are always going astray, and *they have not known my ways.*' So I declared an oath in my anger, 'They shall *never enter my rest.'"* (Heb 3:10-11Emphasis added) Because the hearts of the people went astray and they did not know His ways, they could not enter His rest. Becoming personally familiar with the Lord's ways brings us into His rest. Jesus said, "learn from me…I will give you rest." (Matt 11:28)

How does God's ways help us enter into His rest? God's ways are the windows into His heart. His ways reflect His value system. When we trust in His ways through obedience, we are valuing what He values and resting in His ability to help us. One way God brings rest is through waiting on Him. David encourages us to "Wait on the LORD; Be of good courage, And He shall strengthen your heart; Wait, I say, on the Lord!" (Ps 27:14 NKJ) Isaiah declares, "For since the world began, no ear has heard, and no eye has seen a God like you, *who works for those who wait for Him!* You welcome those who cheerfully do good, *who follow godly ways.*" (Is 64:4 NLT Emphasis added)

We are instructed to work from the posture of rest. Communion with Him always comes first in God's economy. Communion helps reverse the humanistic thought process making it easier to operate in His kingdom. As self-centered human beings, our point of view naturally begins with wanting our needs, desires, and problems to be solved. As a result, we set goals, plan strategies, and chart the purpose for our ministry based on our needs. Instead of waiting on God in prayer for direction, we rely on ourselves by trusting in our education, strength and talent. The only part prayer usually plays in this whole process is to ask God to bless our strategy and work.

Until we set aside our reliance on every human resource and learn to seek God in prayer as the number one priority in life, we will produce only what man can do and miss the Lord's guidance, vision, and supernatural power that changes lives.

We must be careful to avoid the temptation to think of prayer as a way to advance in ministry. Prayer can become a method to merely obtain the anointing we desire in order to be successful. Prayer, first and foremost, provides a way to know the Lord. Henri Nouwen succinctly reminds us to beware of using prayer as a utility tool for ministry instead of a pathway to a deeper relationship with God:

> "Prayer is not merely a condition for compassionate leadership: it is its essence. As long as we keep speaking about prayer as a way to restore ourselves from spiritual fatigue, or worse, to recharge our batteries, we have reduced prayer to a method and compassion to a commodity. Reminding each other that we should not forget to pray in our busy lives is like reminding each other to keep breathing!
>
> Prayer is the essence of the spiritual life without which all ministry loses its meaning. It is the fulfillment of the great commandment to love the Lord our God with all our heart, all our soul, and all our mind. Our heart, soul, and mind can never be divided between God and neighbor. God is a jealous God who wants our love without any reservations. But in our total, undivided commitment to God, God is revealed

to us as the God of our neighbor and so makes our love for God a love that embraces all people in time and place."[4]

Martha and Mary represent two choices. Martha chose to work for Jesus; Mary chose to be with Jesus. Martha's choice kept her at a distance; Mary's moved her nearer to God. Martha's choice produced worry and anxiety; Mary's choice positioned her to learn from Jesus and to enter His rest. From the posture of rest, anything is possible. As Jesus said, "I am the vine; you are the branches. If a man remains in me and I in him, he will bear much fruit; *apart from me* you can do nothing." (Jn. 15:5 Emphasis added)

A PRAYER FOR INTIMACY

Lord Jesus, I am asking for a conversion. Help me to become more like Mary. I no longer want to be one that works for You at a distance, but one who knows Your heart and moves when You move, speaks when You speak, and goes where You go.

So often when You knock on the door of my heart, I don't understand what You are looking for. I find it hard to believe that You knock for the sole purpose of fellowship. I get so distracted, I often jump up to do a task and leave You sitting there, alone, waiting for me. Why do I find tasks so important that I allow them to draw me away from You?

Jesus, like Mary, I want to make the "better choice." The choices that move me continually closer to You and not those that keep me at a safe distance from You. Lord, I want to be near You and know Your heart. I am aware that Your thoughts are not my thoughts, neither are my ways Your ways. Your thoughts and ways are so different from mine. Jesus, teach me Your ways so that I can learn Your heart and enter Your rest. Help me to always remember that when I abide in Your presence it brings rest to my soul.

Jesus, most importantly, help me to draw near to You with a heart that is motivated by Your love for me. Amen!

Chapter Three

Discovering The Relational God

"Our ordinary views of prayer are not found in the New Testament. We look upon prayer as a means for getting something for ourselves; the Bible idea of prayer is that we may get to know God Himself."
Oswald Chambers

A.W. Tozer wisely wrote, "What comes into our minds when we think about God is the most important thing about us."[1] How do you see God? Is He an aloof, abstract being? A judge who demands strict adherence to rules? A gentle grandfather? An unapproachable king? Or, is He a loving father calling you into a deep relationship through outrageous acts of love?

The way we see God is rooted in our life experiences. However, our heavenly Father, who is reflected in the person of Jesus Christ, looks and acts differently than the god that has been formed in our minds by our experiences. We all carry with us misconceptions about God. Unfortunately, when we become Christians, we do not automatically erase these "old" ideas. Our faulty beliefs will hang on until they are confronted with the truth. In the meantime, they can interfere with our ability to draw closer to God. Are you willing to have your self-made views of God challenged? Are you ready to really know God? As unhelpful as they are, some of us would rather keep our familiar views of God because they are more comfortable and manageable. The heavenly Father, creator of all things, is a lot different than the one created through our life experiences.

My view of God was largely shaped by an incident that occurred in my childhood. At the age of nine, my five brothers and sisters and I were removed from our home and placed in an orphanage due to neglect by our parents. I will always remember that day. It was a clear sunny day in August. My brothers and I were returning home from playing in the neighborhood park when we saw an ambulance and a sheriff's car in front of our house. As we raced towards the house, my mother was placed in the ambulance. Before I had a chance to make sense of what was going on, my sisters were put in a car and driven away. My brothers and I were put into another car by social workers and taken to a home where we were cleaned up, our old ragged clothes were thrown away and our hair cut. The next day the social workers returned. They put us all in a sheriff's car and drove us to an orphanage across state. The world as I knew it was forever changed. My parents were not dead, but were unfit to be parents. My father was an alcoholic and constantly got into trouble with the law, ending up in prison. My mother had fallen into a deep depression, rarely getting out of bed during the last several months we were with her. My brothers, sisters and I took care of each other the best we could. We were basically on our own which the authorities discovered after several neglect reports had been filed by neighbors. My mother was placed in a mental institution, never to be reunited with us again.

Out of my childhood experiences, I formed a life philosophy which could be summed up as: "Life is hard then you die." My philosophy of life was rooted in the bitter experiences of rejection, abuse, and hurt encountered at an early age. Without realizing it, I formed conclusions about life and God which I considered to be truth. My experience taught me that if God was real, He must be indifferent to my pain. His apparent indifference caused me to question His love for me and my family. If He really loved us, I reasoned, He would have stopped the abuse and kept my family together. God was either indifferent or didn't exist. This was my way of making sense out of the hurt and trauma life had dealt me. At times, these ideas may have served as a buffer and helped me survive. Ultimately, they became strongholds of distorted thinking that kept me at a distance from experiencing God's love.

Even after personally encountering God's love at the age of twenty, my old concepts of God did not dissolve easily. Adding to these distortions were educational and religious experiences which did not support the idea that a relationship with God was possible. For many of us, erroneous beliefs are not easily identified and replaced with the true knowledge of God. It may take years before we recognize errors in our thinking and realize the depth of relationship we've been missing. It is a process. The apostle Paul described it well when he urged us to "not conform any longer to the pattern of this world." What Paul described as "the pattern of the world" refers to the world view we ascribe to, which is formed by our life experiences as well as religious systems. Paul urges us to be "transformed by the renewing of [our] minds." It is only when this transformation occurs that we are able to understand and receive the attributes of God: His love, His mercy, His grace and as Paul notes, "... His good, pleasing and perfect will." (Rom 12:2)

Formed concepts of God often get in the way of enjoying the wonderful, intimate relationship God offers us through the person of Jesus Christ. The "patterns of the world" subtly influence our heart's decisions without our awareness. Limited by our understanding of God and of ourselves, we may unwittingly embrace these misconstrued concepts of God. On the other hand, when we imagine God to be what He is not, we may attempt to distance ourselves from Him. For example, if we perceive God as judgmental and angry, we may either justify our own judgments and anger, or rebel against Him and accept those things that God Himself does not accept. Either way, this concept of God will affect the course of our lives.

Since our concept of God affects our relationship with Him, naturally it determines how we pray to Him. Prayer is the expression of our relationship with God. Unfortunately, it is difficult if not impossible to have a good relationship with God if we define Him on our terms. A distorted and confused impression of God will lead to a distorted response to Him.

It may provide some comfort to know that we are not alone in struggling with distorted ideas about God's character. For centuries, people have wrestled with the notion of understanding who God is. The seventeenth century French mathematician Blaise Pascal wrestled with faulty concepts about God in his day, noting, "God is not the God of the philosophers…" When he spoke of the god of the philosophers, he referred to a non-personal abstract omni-being. Most people find it difficult to relate to a nameless, faceless philosophical abstraction! Even the religious Pharisees didn't have it quite right. They viewed God as an austere judge who kept records of every infraction against His law, demanding slavish obedience to His rules in order to be accepted.

To discover who God is, we need to examine the life and person of Jesus. The Bible says that Jesus is the image of God (Col 1:15) and the Word of God (Jn 1:1). However, the disciple Philip had difficulty grasping the notion that Jesus was God even after walking with Jesus for over three years. Philip asked Jesus to show him God the Father, as if God the Father were a separate entity. Jesus responded, "Don't you know Me, Philip, even after I have been among you such a long time? Anyone who has seen Me has seen the Father." (Jn 14:9) The only place where we can see an accurate picture of the Father is in the One who is His Word, His image, the sole expression of His glory, and the perfect imprint of His character. All concepts of God must be understood and interpreted in the light of Jesus.

By clinging to old distorted ideas about God, we are not unlike the man in Jesus' parable who out of fear buried the talent given to him by his master. We bury priceless opportunities to experience the unconditional love of God through prayer. In this story, the man told his master he had chosen to bury his talent because, in his words, "I knew that you are a hard man, harvesting where you have not sown and gathering where you have not scattered seed." (Matt 25:24) If we view the Lord as a hard task master, expecting perfection just beyond our reach, we will shrink back from a real encounter with Him. We may respect Him, but from a distance. We may possibly honor and revere Him, but most likely out of joyless fear. Motivated by our need for acceptance, we may want to please Him by trying to live by His standards. In short, a distorted view of God can create a relationship based on fear and performance.

As we continue throughout life, we often interpret various teachings about God from the initial concept we developed of Him. In my case, the view I held of God was one of an aloof judge, indifferent to pain. Even after believing in Him, I continued to value God's holiness and judgment above all else. Initially, I served Him as a servant rather than as a child who obeyed out of love. As a pastor for over twenty five years, I have encountered numerous people who struggle with this same opinion of God. While there are many distorted ideas about God, the "judging or aloof God" view is the one I'd like to address due to its prevalence in the church today.

Approximately fifteen years after receiving Jesus as my

savior, I began to slowly question my perspective concerning God's holiness. Due to the fear-based relationship I had developed with God, I took His absolute perfection of moral excellence to mean that His holiness was the motivation behind all that He said and did. Naturally, as I engaged on a deeper level with the stories in the bible, His actions towards fallen mankind seemed mysterious and somewhat baffling. For example, why did God remove Adam and Eve from the Garden of Eden when they sinned, yet allowed them to live and fill the earth with fallen human beings? Why didn't He destroy them and start over? Their rebellion should have caused them to forfeit their right to the gift of life. Why would God put up with a fallen human race? The mystery that baffled me was that God pursued Adam and Eve in spite of their rebellion and attempt to hide from Him.

It wasn't a surprise to me that a Holy God extinguished most of mankind through the great flood. The Scriptures state, "The earth was depraved and putrid in God's sight, and the land was filled with violence (desecration, infringement, outrage, assault, and lust for power). And God looked upon the world and saw how degenerate, debased, and vicious it was, for all humanity had corrupted their way upon the earth and lost their true direction." (Gen 6:11-12 AMP) In my mind, the state of the earth had succumbed to the simple law of sowing and reaping. You get what you deserve. I had latched onto other scriptures that reinforced this view, such as, "Do not be deceived: God cannot be mocked. A man reaps what he sows. The one who sows to please his sinful nature, from that nature will reap destruction…" (Gal 6:7-8)

Even as God judged His people, it is evident He also went to great lengths to save them. Why, I wondered, did He save Noah and his family, thereby rescuing the human race from extinction? There are countless examples throughout the Bible in which mankind clearly violated God's holy law and yet God did not deal instantly with them according to His strict holy standard. This led me to wonder, "is there something else motivating and influencing God's actions besides His holiness?"

In reading the Bible, what perplexed me was that a Holy God not only desired fellowship with His people but also chased after them. How could that be? My experience had been that "holy" people separated themselves from "unholy" people, cutting off any form of association with them. So, why would a Holy God pursue unholy creatures like us?

The word "holiness" emphasizes everything I am not. It exposes my deficits, insecurities, and failures. Even if God desires fellowship with me, how can I fellowship with Him when I am so conscious of my own flaws? Despite the fact that a holy God has every reason to judge mankind harshly, it turns out that He is extraordinarily patient with all of us. Since the rebellion of Adam and Eve mankind has experienced God's longsuffering, His patience, and His grace, not His justice. These character traits of God were not a part of my old concept of who God was or how He acted. Time and again, the Bible portrays God as delaying His just judgment. But why? Is there another concern on God's heart other than justice? The apostle Peter gives us a hint, "The Lord is not slack concerning His promise, as some count slackness, but is longsuffering toward us, not willing that any should perish but that all should come to repentance." (2 Pet 3:9 NKJ)

If we examine closely the way God reveals Himself in the bible, we will see that God has always been a personal God. From the beginning of creation, God has relentlessly pursued a relationship with His people. His desire for us is seen in the way He introduces Himself. He referred to Himself as "I". God wants His people to know His names because they describe His character. One of the names He wants to be known by is "Yahweh" the "compassionate and gracious God, slow to anger, abounding in love and faithfulness, maintaining love to thousands, and forgiving..." (Ex 34:6) This is intensely personal. He also reveals Himself in terms such as "shepherd" (Ps 80:1) and "husband" (Jer 31:32).

The greatest revelation that God is a personal God is found in the person of Jesus Christ. J. Rodman Williams describes this amazing incarnation:

> "Since God has incarnated Himself in the person of Jesus Christ, this affirms that personal reality is the true expression of divine being... In the ministry of Jesus Christ His every contact with people was extremely personal. His was a life of entering into fellowship, meeting people in their deepest needs, identifying Himself with them even to His death on the cross. Furthermore, Jesus instructed His disciples to call God "Father" and depicted His and their relation to God as that of sons."[2]

Jesus brought the supreme revelation of God's character by the way He lived out His relationship with the Father. His relationship with God the Father was real, genuine, personal, and deeply intimate. Jesus testified about His unique relationship with the Father, saying "No one has seen the Father except the one who is from God; only he has seen the Father." (Jn 6:46) Jesus talked to His Father frequently and with familiarity. He said, "Righteous Father, though the world does not know you, I know you, and they know that you have sent me." (Jn 17:25)

Jesus' relationship with the Father also reveals a unique and mysterious aspect of God's nature, which is the Holy Spirit. Jesus showed us that God is tri-personal or a Trinity. God is Father, Son, and Holy Spirit. The triune God or Trinity is the most fundamental aspect of God.

It is difficult to comprehend that in the One true God there are three distinguishable persons, yet inseparable in essence. The Trinity describes what God is like in Himself, getting to the heart of what motivates Him.Understanding this is beyond our human comprehension; therefore, what we know of God must come through divine revelation. The revelation of the Trinity is clearly revealed in the life of Christ but not fully explained. For example, at Jesus' baptism we see He was not alone but that the Father and the Spirit were actively involved in the event. (See Matt 3:16-17) "For the Trinity is God: God is the Trinity," says Julian of Norwich. "The Trinity is our protector, the Trinity is our everlasting lover, the Trinity is our endless joy and bliss, by our Lord Jesus Christ and in our Lord Jesus Christ.

Where Jesus appears, the blessed Trinity is understood."[3] Julian of Norwich is right. We can only understand the Trinity in and through our Lord Jesus Christ. The heart and life of the Trinity is made known to us through the way God reveals Himself in the person of Jesus Christ. Likewise, the Trinity reveals the core of what motivates God. The Trinity explains the God of love. Love reveals the dynamic characteristics of the Trinity. The core of our faith is composed of the Trinity and love. Therefore, we cannot understand the power of God's love apart from the Trinity. To understand this dynamic of love within the Trinity is to know what type of fellowship to which we have been invited. Christ is our only link between the fellowship of the Trinity and fallen humanity. In light of this, with reverent awe, let us glimpse behind the veil into the very heart of God. Let us behold the heart of the Trinity as revealed in Christ.

What we see in the Trinity is a synergistic shared life, life that is abundantly full and not empty; extravagantly rich and not boring; full of beauty and not sad or lonely. God in Himself is a circle of life, passion and dynamic fellowship. In the fellowship of the Trinity there is passionate life, purity of light and selfless love. In this vibrant relationship between the Father, Son, and Holy Spirit there is no legalism; there are no religious rules and no regulations. In this relationship of light and love there is only freedom. Father, Son and Holy Spirit are totally free to be themselves because they are totally and eternally pure. Their love is devoid of any ulterior motives. In rare moments of intimacy with others, we may encounter glimpses of this love. This "dynamic" is often experienced as a paradox. For example, in the midst of overwhelming grief, we might sense God's compassion and closeness more deeply than ever before. In the act of forgiving or receiving forgiveness, we may become united with that individual in a deeper way. At the birth of a child, we often experience the sensation of our heart expanding and overflowing with a love never deemed possible. These paradoxical glimpses remove the boundaries that have been set by our human definitions and codes. At times, what is experienced makes no sense and yet makes perfect sense. As we open ourselves to knowing God as He describes Himself, surprisingly, we will find we are able to embrace the mystery of the Trinity, without completely understanding it. We were made in the image of the triune God; therefore the reality and command to love are "Imago Dei" (the image of God) realities. We were made to receive and give love the way God gives and receives love.

Given that God is triune and at the very essence of His being love, the very core of His heart is relational. God has never been alone. Before any creature was created, there always was togetherness, communion, and fellowship of the three personalities in the Godhead. In eternity past, God has always existed in relationship. The Trinity exists in communion and a vibrant interactive life.

Once we accept that God is triune and relational, God will begin to dissolve our old concepts of Him. We must shed these like "old wineskin" ideas in order to "put on" the correct concept of who God is. We should never underestimate how ingrained our ideas can be! My mental image of holiness, though clearly too narrow and too limited, was difficult to shake. In the light of the tri-personality of God, holiness is not merely describing a righteous moral standard but a vibrant way of life. It describes the quality of God's life. God's dynamic life is whole, clean, right, and full of joy, peace and harmony. God is light and there is no darkness in Him. Holiness points to God being true, faithful, and just. (See James 1:17, 1 John 1:5) Although it is difficult to completely grasp the holiness of God, we can choose to view it not in isolation but in the multi-faceted relationship of the Trinity. Holiness describes the dynamic wonder and the amazing beauty in how God relates to Himself (Father, Son, and Holy Spirit) and to His creation.

In addition, "The meaning of God's holiness is completed in the meaning of His love," said Albert Truesdale. "And the meaning of His love is completed in His holiness. Unless these two are kept in balance, God's holiness may be distorted into a harsh, threatening transcendence, and His love may dissipate into aimless sentimentality." These two attributes describe who God is. Holiness and love are like a multi-faceted diamond. From one angle they seem to complement each other, yet from another point of view, one fulfills the demands of the other. However from a different perspective they seem to be at odds, threatening to tear each other apart, but find themselves kissing at the cross of Christ. While appearing contradictive, holiness and love exist in unity in the Godhead.

Love and holiness are alive and working together in harmony in the life of Christ. It is in Jesus Christ that divine love and holiness are defined, revealed, and expressed. In Christ, love and holiness are moved from the abstract to the tangible, from the ideal to the real. Everything Jesus taught He lived. Jesus is incarnate Holy Love. Holiness is not an impersonal ethical moral code contained in rules. Moral codes are inflexible and rigid. Purity and love are the core components of holiness displayed by Jesus. The Father's will for our lives is to become Christ-like and not law-like. Instead of us conforming to a principle, we are conforming to a person. Instead of following an idea, we are following Jesus. The true heart of God is revealed in Jesus as an infinite heart of holy love.

Jesus being incarnate holy love lived His life in a dynamic love relationship with the Father. The Father spoke from heaven saying, "This is my Son, whom I love; with him I am well pleased." (Matt 3:17) Jesus said, "The world must learn that I love the Father and that I do exactly what my Father has commanded me." (Jn 14:31) Jesus' love for the Father and the Father's love for Jesus was the foundation of their communion with each other.

Jesus and the Father are in constant fellowship with each other; therefore He was never alone or on His own. Jesus said, *"The one who sent me is with me; he has not left me alone*, for I always do what pleases him." (Jn 8:29 Emphasis added) Jesus told the Jews in John 10:38 to believe His miracles so "that you may know and understand that *the Father is in me, and I in the Father.*" (Emphasis added) In the upper room discourse with His disciples, Jesus said, "Don't you believe that I am in the Father, and that the Father is in me? The words I say to you are not just my own. Rather, it is the *Father, living in me*, who is doing his work." (Jn 14:10 Emphasis added) Jesus not only had unbroken fellowship with the Father, but was also totally dependent on the Holy Spirit. Before entering into ministry Jesus received the Holy Spirit without measure. "Jesus, full of the Holy Spirit, returned from the Jordan and was led by the Spirit in the desert…" (Lk 4:1-2)

Since Jesus loved the Father and was in constant fellowship with Him, Jesus never acted alone. His speech and actions revealed His dependence on and fellowship with the Father and the Spirit. Luke informs us that Jesus talked to the Father through the Spirit: "Jesus, full of joy through the Holy Spirit, said, "I praise you, Father, Lord of heaven and earth"..." (Lk 10:21) Jesus said, "I tell you the truth, the Son can do nothing by himself; he can do only what he sees his Father doing, because whatever the Father does the Son also does. For the Father loves the Son and shows him all he does." (Jn 5:19-20)

Given that Jesus always enjoyed the loving fellowship of the Father and Spirit, and never acted on His own, His love was alive with the fullness of the Trinitarian life. Jesus' love for us is not separate from the Father's love nor is it merely a likeness or reflection of the Father's love. His love includes the Father's love. Jesus said "My sheep listen to my voice; I know them, and they follow me. I give them eternal life, and they shall never perish; no one can snatch them out of my hand.

My Father, who has given them to me, is greater than all; no one can snatch them out of my Father's hand. I and the Father are one." (Jn 10:27-30) The Son's hand of love and the Father's hand of love work in unity. We see the oneness of Christ and the Father in the revelation of their protective love.

The essence of the triune love was revealed when Christ died for us on the cross. This selfless, giving, other-orientated love revealed a sacrificial quality to its nature when Jesus went to the cross. "You see, at just the right time, when we were still powerless, Christ died for the ungodly. Very rarely will anyone die for a righteous man, though for a good man someone might possibly dare to die. But God demonstrates his own love for us in this: While we were still sinners, Christ died for us." (Rom 5:6-8) His sacrificial love has a depth to it that is unsurpassable. Jesus did not die for a righteous man or a good man but for sinners who are rebels and God haters. He died for His enemies. In this act of dying for us, Jesus valued our lives more than His own, ascribing unsurpassable worth to us. (See Phil 2:3) Jesus who has eternal value, bestowed that same value on us when He took our place on the cross. This display of love shows the perfect love that exists between the Father, Son, and Holy Spirit.

A greater depth of His love was revealed when Jesus, the spotless lamb of God, the righteous King, the perfect Son took upon Himself our sin. Our sin is repulsive and opposite to His very nature, yet He became our sin in order to redeem us to Himself. Paul writes "For He made Him who knew no sin to be sin for us, that we might become the righteousness of God in Him." (2 Cor 5:21) The dazzling beauty of love revealed in Christ dying for His enemies reveals the stunning beauty of love within the triune fellowship.

The sacrificial love that is revealed in the cross has always been an eternal dynamic principle in the love of God. It is inherent in the heart of God. "We see then the Cross is far more than an act in history," writes Devern Fromke. "It expresses the very qualities and manner of life of the triune God. It is the life-giving, light-sharing and love-bestowing principle by which God has dealt with man from the beginning."[4] The cross is a picture of the life-giving, light-sharing and love-bestowing heart of the Trinity.

The Father is love and because He is love He is inviting us to commune with Him through Jesus Christ by His Spirit. The cords of His love are drawing us into His liberating and life-giving fellowship. The Father is calling us to shed our misconceptions of Him which keep us from truly pursuing Him. God is not afraid of our doubts or questions. He knows that our minds are not capable of grasping or comprehending the mystery of His being. Nevertheless, He is inviting us to embrace Him by faith with all of our heart.

During the past several years, there have been seasons when I felt drawn to read and meditate on the Gospel of John, especially on the upper room discourse in chapters 13–17. During one of these seasons, I struggled for months to comprehend what the Lord was imparting in this passage. Personalizing the Lord's dialogue in the Gospel of John helped me to understand the revelation of God as Father, Son, and Holy Spirit. The majority of the revelation regarding the Trinity is revealed in the Gospel of John. Personalizing scripture in prayer places you directly before the Lord, creating the sense that He is talking specifically to you. This method can facilitate the process of grasping new truths and revelations about God. In order to receive the broader revelation of who God is, it is important to remember to not only comprehend with our minds, but also to embrace the truth with our hearts. The revelation of the knowledge of God is not meant to be merely studied. It is designed to move us deeper into God. The following is a composite of dialogues between God and I which I composed while reading through those passages. Perhaps it will help you begin your own dialogue with God to discover who He is and how He loves you. Hopefully it will assist you in opening your heart to embrace what your mind cannot completely comprehend.

A PRAYER FOR INTIMACY

My Prayer

O Lord, I didn't think You cared. You seemed indifferent to my pain. I imagined You as a hard task master demanding perfection I could not produce. To me, You were an emotionless austere judge who looked upon my weakness in a disapproving manner. The disappointments I experienced during my childhood lead me to distrust people, projecting their unfaithfulness on You, imagining

You to be untrustworthy like them. Since I did not trust You, it was safer to keep You at a distance. However, Your constant loving pursuit for my heart, proved me wrong! You are faithful and trustworthy! Forgive me for clinging to the incorrect beliefs about Your character. Draw me closer to You. My desire is to completely trust You. Show me the depth of Your love so I may truly know You.

Jesus Replied

"I will show you the full extent of My love, revealing My Father's heart to you. No one has ever seen My Father but Me, God the Son, who is always at the Father's side. My Father and I are one. If you have seen Me you have seen My Father. I am in the Father, and the Father is in Me. The words I say to you are not My own. It is the Father living in Me, who is doing His work. Believe Me when I say that I am in the Father and the Father is in Me."

My Prayer

It is difficult to comprehend what You are telling me! I don't understand how You and the Father can be one, yet two separate persons.

Jesus Replied

"I know these words may not make sense to you but I am revealing My love when I disclose the relationship I have with My Father. Love is an eternal dynamic relationship of sharing and giving. Though you cannot completely understand this with your mind, I am asking you to believe Me with your heart. If you cannot trust the testimony about Me and My Father, then at least let the miracles I do in My Father's name convince you. My teaching is not My own. It comes from My Father who sent Me. If you are willing to do His will from your heart then you will certainly know what I say is the truth."

My Prayer

Jesus, You lived in heaven's glory, yet you became the Son of man in order to bring the treasures of heaven's love to me. By showing God's love, You revealed to me the Father and the Holy Spirit. You have invited me into the circle of Your love. I believe Your testimony about Yourself and Your Father for no one has spoken the way You do. My heart is Yours. I am willing to do Your will.

Jesus Replied

"The Father, the Holy Spirit, and I are one. Whatever We do We do together in unity. My Father and I love you. Our love works together in unity for you. No one can snatch you out of Our hands. You are secure in Our embrace."

My Prayer

O my Lord, You are a mystery. I asked You to show me more of Your love and You revealed the rich relationship You and the Father share. You revealed God as the high and exalted One who inhabits eternity and whose name is Holy, as my Father. You are amazingly personal! You revealed Yourself to me opening the door for me to engage in intimate fellowship with my Father. No one has ever seen God, but You, Jesus, have revealed Him to my heart.

Jesus Replied

"The same way the Father has loved Me, I love you. I love you with the same intensity and measure. I love you with My whole heart holding nothing back. Now come, live in My love. If you follow My teaching, My love will become your home. I will surround you with the cords of My love, drawing you closer and closer. I have shared these things with you so that My joy may be in you and your joy may be overflowing."

My Prayer

Your love, Father, is amazing! Thank You for igniting my heart with your passionate love. Jesus, thank You for demonstrating to me the abundant life and selfless love of my Father.

Amen!

CHAPTER FOUR

The Pursuing Lover

"Accustom yourself to the wonderful thought that God loves you with a tenderness, a generosity, and an intimacy which surpasses all your dreams. Give yourself up with joy to a loving confidence in God and have courage to believe firmly that God's action towards you is a masterpiece of partiality and love. Rest tranquilly in this abiding conviction."

ABBE HENRI DE TOURVILLE (1842-1903)

A little boy was playing in his backyard one day when he heard the sound of a buzz saw. Curious, he followed the sound through a gap in his fence and ended up at a construction site of a new home on a nearby lot. There amidst towering stacks of plywood, gleaming metal piping and tools of all shapes and sizes, he encountered a mason mixing sand, water and gray powder. "What are you doing?" he asked the man. The mason replied, "I am making mortar so that I can lay these bricks together." Next, the boy came upon a carpenter wielding a hammer and asked him, "What are you doing?" The carpenter told him, "I am hammering this nail into this piece of wood." The boy then met a plumber who described his task this way: "I am gluing these pipes together so there will be water at this house." Finally, the boy approached a man looking closely at a set of drawings. "What are you doing?" he asked. The man looked down at the little boy and said, "I am building a new home for my family, a place where we can rest, eat, play and enjoy each other." In this scene, the first three men describe a specific task. The fourth man sees the big picture. The first three relate information about a job. The fourth explains the ultimate purpose for the job. For the mason, the carpenter, and the plumber the construction project is a source of employment. For the other man, it is his home.

When it comes to prayer, many of us are like the workers in this story; we view prayer as a simple and sometimes utilitarian religious activity. Many of us may work diligently at prayer—focusing on its form, style or method—but miss its ultimate purpose, which is to draw closer to God. Once we view God as the Trinity and the essence of His being as love, we will begin to value the relational aspect of prayer. The man, Christ Jesus, who is the author and architect of our faith, reveals the blueprint for prayer. When we encounter Jesus, the lover of our soul, prayer will no longer be a mere task but rather a form of communion.

What is the big picture? To understand God's intention for prayer it is necessary to start at the beginning. God's motivation throughout time has been to commune with us. Before the dawn of time there was only God the Father, Son, and Holy Spirit sharing a dynamic life of love, joy, and fellowship. No space, no time, no dimension, no material, no creature, only God existed. The Trinity decided to create human beings in their image, so that mankind could participate in Their wonderful fellowship of life, love, joy, knowledge and creativity. Moses described this when he said, "Then God said, 'Let *us* make man in *our* image, in *our* likeness... So God created man in his own image, in the image of God he created him; male and female he created them.'" (Gen 1:26-27 Emphasis added) Birthed from the loving fellowship of the Trinity, came the decision to create human beings. It's mystifying as to why the Father, Son, and Holy Spirit would decide to create us in their image. In so doing, they enable us to have the capacity to enjoy Their selfless love through communion and fellowship with Them.

Think about this! From the beginning of time you and I have been the object of selfless love. What a powerful thought, beyond most imaginations! To grasp it, we must throw out common erroneous perceptions regarding the reason God created mankind. God did not fashion us because He needed servants. Man was not created because God craved worship. Neither were loneliness and companionship the motivation behind our creation. God is not needy! The Father was completely satisfied with the eternal companionship that existed between Himself, the Son, and the Holy Spirit. God wasn't under any compulsion to create due to a deficit within Himself. (See Acts 17:24-25)

So why did He create us? The prophet Jeremiah records: "The Lord appeared to us in the past, saying: 'I have loved you with an everlasting love; I have drawn you with loving-kindness.'" (Jer 31:3) God created us out of extravagant love overflowing from His relationship with the Son and the Holy Spirit. He created us with the potential capacity to possess His love and character—His wisdom, righteousness, truth, mercy, compassion, power and His authority. One of God's most amazing gifts is to be a vessel of His love.

God's ultimate purpose for creation becomes more evident as the Father's relationship with the Son is examined. In the last chapter we learned that the Father loves the Son and the Son loves the Father. The interplay between the Father and the Son is one of infinite delight rooted in infinite love. The Father revealed His delight in His Son at Jesus' baptism: "And a voice from heaven said, 'This is my Son, whom I love; with him I am well pleased.'"(Matt 3:17)

On the Mt. of Transfiguration, the Father's love for Jesus was once again confirmed: "While he was still speaking, a bright cloud enveloped them, and a voice from the cloud said, 'This is my Son, whom I love; with him I am well pleased. Listen to him!'" (Matt 17:5) In these Scriptures the Father publicly displayed His affection for His Son. He was not ashamed to tell the world how much He delighted in His Son.

God the Father, who has unspeakable delight in His Son, Jesus, longs to have more sons and daughters with whom He can share His love. His desire and purpose is to have a vast family of Spirit (God)-filled human sons and daughters who become just like His only begotten Son. The Apostle Paul provides a look into the eternal heart of God when He tells us that God the Father "chose us in Him [Christ] before the foundation of the world, that we should be holy and without blame before Him in love, having predestined us to *adoption as sons* by Jesus Christ *to Himself*, according to the good pleasure of His will…" (Eph 1:4-5 NKJV Emphasis added) Eugene Peterson translates the passage this way: "Long before he laid down earth's foundations, he had us in mind, *had settled on us as the focus of his love, to be made whole and holy by his love.* Long, long ago he decided to adopt us into his family through Jesus Christ. (What pleasure he took in planning this!) He wanted us to enter into the celebration of his lavish gift-giving by the hand of his beloved Son." (Eph 1:2-5 MSG Emphasis added)

God's purpose for the creation and redemption of mankind is placed in an eternal dimension by this verse. His purpose reaches back in time before the fall of mankind and even before creation itself. God is the eternal Father; He always has been and always will be. Taking a closer look at the phrase "to Himself," it shows that God's love is drawing us back to Him. The reason why God went to the expense of redeeming mankind to Himself is because He desired to complete what He started in the Garden of Eden. Before the world began, His soul intent was to enter into a Father/child relationship with His creation that would bear His image in order to pour out His unsurpassable delight and unconditional love.

In the book of Proverbs, the scriptures paint a beautiful picture of the Trinity working together to create mankind. Each member of the Trinity was actively and delightfully involved. In Proverbs 8:30-31, Wisdom (personified) is revealed as being with God during creation. "Then I was the craftsman at his side. I was filled with delight day after day, rejoicing always in his presence, rejoicing in his whole world and delighting in mankind." This scripture is speaking of Jesus who is the wisdom of God. John 1:1-3 discloses Jesus as the Word: "in the beginning was the Word, and the Word was with God, and the Word was God. He was with God in the beginning. Through him all things were made; without him nothing was made that has been made." (Also see Heb 1:2, Col 1:16) In addition, the New Testament reveals that in the incarnate Son of God are hidden all the treasures of wisdom and knowledge. (Col 2:3) He is expressed as the wisdom of God. (1 Cor 1:24)

The Son and the Father were rejoicing over mankind, knowing Jesus would be the first born among many brothers in whom He would not be ashamed. (See Rom 8:29-30, Heb 2:11-12) The Father also delighted with the Son in Their creation since They intended for the Son to have an eternal companion, described by the Apostle John as "the bride, the Lamb's wife." (Rev 2:19) The Holy Spirit, in celebration with the Father, has the joyful role of revealing the Father's love to the hearts of His people. By dwelling in His people, the Holy Spirit exercises God's unconditional love by empowering, motivating, guiding, and helping them to be sons and daughters of the Father. He inspires God's children by uncovering the genuine cry of "Abba Father" in their hearts. In partnership with Jesus, the Spirit also has the opportunity to inflame the heart of the Bride of Christ, the church, with the perfect love of God for the Son of God as the Bridegroom. As a trio, The Father, Son and Holy Spirit delight over the fact that the Spirit dwells not only in individual hearts but also in the living temple which is called the Body of Christ. (See I Cor 3:16)

When God created Adam and Eve, He expressed His joy and pleasure by proclaiming His creation to be "very good." (Gen 1:31) The shared intent of the Father, the Son, and the Holy Spirit was to draw mankind into the circle of Their love to share in Their joy and delight. We exist for the Father, Son and Holy Spirit to extend Their life and love to us. Therefore, if we accept that God created us out of love, we will begin to view God as a relational Father.

For God to truly relate to us in love, He had to create us with a free will. Without this we cannot truly receive and give love. To be free to love means we are also free to reject love. The story of Adam and Eve illustrates this concept. God created Adam and Eve placing them in the Garden of Eden which contained two trees representing two choices, life or death. Out of their free will, Adam and Eve rejected God by choosing the tree of knowledge of good and evil. In so doing, they severed their relationship with God, accepting Satan's illusionary lie of freedom. Sadly, instead of freedom, they found bondage. They became disconnected and alienated from one another and God.

Even after mankind's rebellion, the intensity of God's loving desire to give Himself to us in love is hard to imagine. Yet, the

Prophet Isaiah spoke of God's passion when he prophesied: "For to us a child is born, to us a son is given, and the government will be on his shoulders… The zeal of the Lord Almighty will accomplish this." (Is 9:6, 7) The word "zeal" contains the idea of glowing fire and creates the picture of an intense passion that is even greater than a person's wrath. It is God's fiery love that compelled Him to become a man.

The arrival of Jesus on earth was not an afterthought on God's part. The Trinity was not caught off guard by the rebellion of the first couple. In the counsel of the Trinity, God the Son was chosen to become a man bringing redemption and the predetermined plan of sharing the dynamic life and love of the Trinity with mankind.

The nature of God's love is sacrificial as revealed in the bible; both the Father and the Son give out of love. "For God [*the Father*] so loved the world that he gave his one and only Son, that whoever believes in him shall not perish but have eternal life. For God [*the Father*] did not send his Son into the world to condemn the world, but to save the world through him." (Jn 3:16-17) The Father's act of sending Christ into the world was an expression of the Father's love for the world. Jesus out of His own voluntary love consented to come to earth as a human being.

God's passion for His people and His sacrificial love is best illustrated in the mystery of the Incarnation. Through the Incarnation, God literally drew close to mankind. The God of Heaven, without ceasing to be God, became flesh. As Timothy put it, "Without question, this is the great mystery of our faith: Christ was revealed in a human body..." (1 Tim 3:16 NLT)

The Incarnation is often viewed with the single mindset that Jesus needed a body so He could die on the cross for our redemption. In essence, we are saying that He was born to die, but perhaps it is more accurate to say He was ultimately born to live with us for eternity. His death provided the means to remove the barrier between us and God so that we could live with Him forever. John proclaimed, "This is how God showed his love among us: He sent his one and only Son into the world that we might live through him." (1 Jn 4:9) Paul states that "It has now been revealed through the appearing of our Savior, Christ Jesus, who has destroyed death and has brought life and immortality to light through the gospel." (2 Tim 1:10)

The Incarnation is the expression of His love, the central drama of our redemption. After Jesus' resurrection, He did not stop being a man. The God-man will always be Jesus of Nazareth the son of Mary. God the Son did not temporarily become a man for a season and then return to heaven, shedding his humanity and going back to just being God. When God the Son chose to become human, it was forever. We need to understand that the Incarnation is God approaching us and dwelling among us. He is Immanuel—God with us—in the person of Jesus Christ.

It is easy to forget this personal God who became a man is also Yahweh. He is God who revealed Himself at Mt. Sinai in a "blazing fire and darkness, gloom and a whirlwind" (Heb.

12:18). People shrunk back in fear from Yahweh. They dreaded God who declared: "If even an animal touches the mountain, it must be stoned." (Heb 12:20) Out of fear, Israel misinterpreted Yahweh's approach. The scriptures tell us that the Israelites "stayed at a distance and said to Moses, 'Speak to us yourself and we will listen. But do not have God speak to us or we will die.'" (Ex 20:18-19) From the people's perspective, God appeared to be unapproachable and inaccessible. Out of fear, they asked Moses to go to God on their behalf. Moses tried to correct their response: "*Do not be afraid.* God has come to test you, so that the fear of God will be with you to keep you from sinning." (Ex 20:20 Emphasis added) It is obvious from the phrase "do not be afraid" that God did not want them to run from Him but to Him in awe, fascination, and reverential worship. In verse 21, we sadly read, "The people remained at a distance, while Moses approached the thick darkness where God was." It was God's intent for the people to draw close to Him, but they did not.

God again took the initiative to approach His people by means of the Incarnation. This time God became accessible to mankind by becoming one of us. God became approachable and even touchable. Jesus approached the sinners, tax gatherers, and the destitute. He let children, lepers, and the sick touch Him. As a result, they were blessed and healed. By becoming a man, God drew near and completely gave Himself to us. What kind of love motivated the Son of God to become a man in order to live forever with mankind? It was an extreme act of love. For God the Son to lay aside His power and glory, subjecting Himself to a mixture of arrogant pride, haughty skepticism and ruthless violence is outrageous! It appears to be shear madness for the all powerful God to make His entrance on earth as a vulnerable, helpless baby. Why would God become a man and subject Himself to such a plan? He was moved by love–unimaginable love–for the human race.

Catherine of Siena described this unimaginable love when she cried out in prayer:

> "Oh, abyss of love! What heart can help breaking when it sees such dignity as yours descend to such lowliness as our humanity? We are your image, and you have become ours, by this union which you have accomplished with man, veiling the eternal Deity with the cloud of woe and the corrupted clay of Adam. For what reason?—Love."[2]

The outrageous act of Christ becoming one of us should move every believer to extravagant worship as it did Catherine of Siena. Her words capture the essence of the Incarnation as a truth that inflames the heart rather than mere doctrine. In understanding this concept our prayers, like those of Catherine of Siena, will become intertwined with worship, reflecting our total relationship with Him.

Interestingly, some find it difficult to move beyond the idea that God was motivated to become a man in order to redeem us from sin and judgment. They receive salvation but miss the big picture. In so doing, they miss the loving invitation to enter a relationship with the Almighty God, creator of the universe! The Father's invitation is to join His family of sons and daughters; the Holy Spirit wants a living temple, which is called the Body of Christ; and Jesus, desires a radiant Bride. These relationships speak of intimate fellowship that pulsates with divine love.

What causes some of us to refuse this offer of intimacy? Perhaps we don't understand it or find it hard to believe. Possibly we fear the change that might need to take place if we accept this invitation. Maybe we feel we are incapable of receiving or giving such love. The truth is we are incapable, but the Holy Spirit is able to help us. When Jesus became a human He brought a new identity to the human race. Bernard of Clairvaux described this identity as: "In [my creation] he gave me myself; in [the incarnation] he gave himself; and when he did that he gave me myself. Given and given again, I owe myself in return for myself, twice over."[3] It is important to understand that Jesus gave us a new self or identity different from the one we received at our natural birth. The core of this new identity is Christ Himself, the Beloved; one who is desired and is outrageously loved by God.

Paul explains, "if anyone is in Christ, he is a new creation; the old has gone, the new has come! All this is from God, who reconciled us to himself through Christ…" (2 Cor 5:17-18) When we give our lives to Christ we become someone we've never been before. A follower of Christ, in terms of His deepest identity, is a new creation. In our relationship with God the Father, we are the Father's beloved sons and daughters. In our relationship with Jesus, we are the Son's beloved Bride. In our relationship with the Holy Spirit, we are His living temple. It is out of this new identity that we can live a new life with God. Through Christ's example on earth, and with the assistance of the Holy Spirit, we can learn how to live this life. Christian author Major Ian Thomas put in this way:

> "He becomes Man as God intended man to be, and behaved as God intended man to behave, walking day by day in that relationship to the Father which God had always intended should exist between man and Himself. In all His [Jesus'] activities, in all His reactions, in every step He took and in every word He said, in every decision He made, He did as *man*, even though He was God. He knew that in His perfection *as man*, the Father had vested in Him all that God intended to vest in man-all things… To put it another way, all the inexhaustible supplies of God are available to the man who is available to all the inexhaustible supplies of God; and Jesus Christ was that man! He was Man in perfection-totally, unrelentingly, unquestioningly available-and that is why there was available to Him all that to which He was available-all things!"[4]

Because Jesus, the perfect man, lived His life in total dependency on the Father and drew His life, strength, and power from the Father, so we too can draw our life source from the Son by being dependent upon Him for everything. (See 2 Peter 1:3) Everything Christ said or did came out of fellowship with His Father. The same is possible for us! Jesus described this way of live when He said, "I tell you the truth, the Son can do nothing by himself; he can do only what he sees his Father doing, because whatever the Father does the Son also does. For the Father loves the Son and shows him all he does." (Jn 5:19-20)

Jesus stated that a life of dependence upon Him comes to "the one who feeds on" Him and he "will live because of me." (Jn 6:57) Jesus has made available to us all the dynamics of the Trinitarian life and love. Perhaps the greatest aspect of fellowship with God is eternal life. Jesus, throughout His ministry, spoke about eternal life, In John 3:16, He said, "For God so loved the world that he gave his one and only Son, that whoever believes in him shall not perish but have eternal life." What is this eternal life that Jesus is offering? Simply put, it is life lived in relationship with Him. Jesus said, "My sheep listen to my voice; I know them, and they follow me. I give them eternal life..." (Jn 10:27) The Greek word for "know" is the same word for knowing by experience. Jesus knows His sheep through a personal relationship with them. In and through that personal relationship Jesus shares Himself. The scripture states, "Now this is eternal life: that they may know you, the only true God, and Jesus Christ, whom you have sent." (Jn 17:3) To "know" is to know through personal experience.

When we think of eternal life, we often think of what happens after we die. In Jesus' definition of eternal life, He instead emphasized a quality of relationship which is outside the boundaries of time. John explains that "God has given us eternal life, and this life is in his Son. He who has the Son has life; he who does not have the Son of God does not have life." (1Jn 5:11-12) We do not have to wait until we die to experience this life; we have it now in our relationship with the Son of God! Jesus declared the purpose of His coming when He said, "I came that they may have and enjoy life, and have it in abundance." (Jn 10:10 AMP) This abundant life overflows to us from the life and love of the Trinity. It's a life lived in fellowship with the Trinity.

Just as the boy in our story met a man who had a vision for a beautiful home in which his family would enjoy each other, we have seen that our Father desires to have a family of spirit-filled sons and daughters who can receive and give His love. Out of His great passion for us, God invites us to literally draw from His vast and powerful love as we live our lives. Without any preconditions or performance, we are invited to live a life rooted and grounded in love. When we do, prayer will not be a religious activity but a form of communion with our Lord.

In Isaiah, the Lord states "Come, all you who are thirsty, come to the waters; and you who have no money, come, buy and eat! Come, buy wine and milk without money and without cost." (Isa 55:1) In Revelation 22:17, Jesus declares "Whoever is thirsty, let him come; and whoever wishes, let him take the free gift of the water of life."

Are we thirsty? Do we desire to have a life rooted in love?

The offer given to us originates from love therefore our response must be one of trust. It is through trusting God that we can participate in a relationship with Him and enjoy the fullness of life He offers. Trust works through love. We can only trust Him to the degree that we have confidence in His love for us.

For many of us, it may come as an amazing yet startling realization that Jesus is giving Himself to us in love. His love is everything we've ever desired or wanted. It may take some time to fully accept the abundant, powerful life of the Trinity Jesus offers. A rich life full of joy, love, harmony, humility, truth, communion and fellowship is offered to us (See John 17:20-23). This life is so dynamic and full of power the Bible compares it to a river. "The river of the water of life, as clear as crystal, flowing from the throne of God and of the Lamb…" (Rev 22:1) Our thirst will not only be quenched by this abundant river of life, but it will also be like streams of living water flowing out from within. (See Jn 7:37-39) Perhaps the first step is to acknowledge we are thirsty and take a sip!

After taking a sip, the revelation of His love will begin to unfold. The next several chapters will reveal how this will affect us and our relationship with Him. We will see that prayer is simply a natural extension of our relationship.

A PRAYER FOR INTIMACY

"O Lord, what is man that you care for him, the son of man that you think of him?"[5]. Life is a mere breath; my days are so temporal they seem to be like a fleeting shadow. Yet, I am the object of Your affection, the focus of Your concern.

Awaken my heart to the fiery zeal of Your love. Open the eyes of my heart so that I can see the intensity of Your love. The love that compelled You to become man so that I can fellowship with You. O Lord, You are the Holy and Transcendent One, but you made Yourself accessible. You are never distant or aloof. You, the living Word, became human and dwelt among us. The glory of the Father's one and only Son, who is full of unfailing love and faithfulness, has been revealed.

It seems that eternal love could not stay in heaven. It was love that brought You down to earth. You set aside the privileges of deity and took on flesh and blood. It was because of love that You humbled Yourself in order to made Yourself approachable, even touchable to sinful man. What depths of humility are rooted in love!

O My Lord Jesus, You are the incarnation of divine love, the compassion of God made visible. You came down to live among us to confront my fears, my guilt, my shame and feelings of emptiness and despair. Living among sinners, You endured my hate, my rejection, and my hard heart. What kind of love is this that even hate and rejection cannot stop it? By Your grace, through faith in You Jesus, I can approach You in my brokenness. I will never be able to totally grasp You with my mind but You allow me to embrace You with my heart.

My heart has been awakened to the amazing revelation of Your love and the abundant life You share with the Father and the Spirit! This life is overflowing with joy, love, harmony, humility, and truth. I desire the life You are offering. Come Lord! Invade my life with Yours! Amen

Chapter Five

The Essence Of Prayer

"You, eternal Trinity, are the craftsman; and I your handiwork have come to know that you are in love with the beauty of what you have made, since you made of me a new creation in the blood of your Son. O abyss! O eternal Godhead! O deep sea! What more could you have given me than the gift of your very self?" Catherine of Sienna

When Jesus came to Bethany, He sought rest and fellowship. He and His disciples were tired from a busy schedule of ministry. Martha, a local resident, invited them in for dinner. Mary, her sister, was curious about this group of men reclining and resting in their home. There was something about Jesus that captured Mary's attention. He was no ordinary guest. Jesus was different from all the other teachers she had heard. What was it? Mary watched and listened. His words! There was something about His words. He spoke with passion about God and life. His words conveyed a depth of reality she had not considered before; she felt as if she understood for the first time what it meant when people spoke of God's compassion, love and mercy. A fire was kindled within her heart by His words. As Mary's heart began to burn, she wanted to hear more but her duty was in the kitchen with her sister Martha preparing the meal.

At first, Mary may have been hesitant; perhaps poking her head into the room where Jesus was to hear what He was saying. Drawn by His words, she entered the room, staying against the wall. But then, Mary's heart was awakened, by His words, to the love of God, and she had to draw closer. In that moment, Mary summoned the courage to ignore the disapproving looks of the disciples and the expectations of her sister to sit at Jesus' feet. In so doing, she broke the social and religious customs of her day.

Mary did not view herself as radical, brave, or revolutionary. When the love of God touched her heart, she did not care what people thought because she knew in that moment what God thought of her. She saw the "hidden treasure" in the field, the immeasurable riches of God revealed in Jesus, and would not allow the social and religious customs to distract her. A revelation of the love of God in Christ touched the very core of her being. As a result, Mary became single-minded in her pursuit to know Christ.

When it comes to defining prayer, the phrase "sitting at Jesus' feet" is one of the best descriptions. It implies, first and foremost, that the Lord is the focus and the center of prayer. Second, it conveys a picture of men and women who, like Mary, are being touched by the revelation of God's love in Christ Jesus. As Mary sat at Jesus' feet, the eyes of her heart opened and she beheld God. At the same time, everything else around her fell out of focus. Mary's experience exemplifies the communion that is possible in prayer. As we experience this intimate "beholding," we, like Mary, will undoubtedly want to draw closer to Christ. The same insatiable hunger to personally know Christ will overtake us. With increased focus and hunger for intimacy, prayer shifts from a long distance phone conversation to an intimate dialogue with our loving Father.

When asked to define prayer, the common answer most people give is "Talking to God." Some of the great Christian writers of the past have also defined prayer in these terms. Clement of Alexandria said, "Prayer is conversation with God." John Knox wrote, "[Prayer is] an earnest and familiar talking with God."[1] Talking to God is basic to prayer and a great start. But, if this is all we understand about prayer, then we have limited ourselves to a narrow practice and experience. Prayer, as revealed in the Bible, is a dialogue, not a monologue. To have a meaningful conversation, both parties need to actively participate. What defines and shapes any dialogue is how we relate to the other person involved. The conversations I have with my wife are totally different than those I might have with a boss. The way I talk to my friends is different than the way I relate to a policeman who has pulled me over for speeding. Understanding our relationship with the Lord is important if we are going to grow in prayer. As discussed earlier, the way we view God plays a central role in our interactions with Him! Our conversations with the Lord are determined by how we view His character and heart in relationship to us. Is God perceived as judgmental and distant or compassionate and merciful? Do we see ourselves as servants or as sons and daughters?

If God is thought to be distant and detached from our daily troubles, prayer becomes primarily used as an urgent cry for help during emergent situations, like a 911 call. The conversation is generated by feelings of panic or fear rather than intimacy. Often the Lord does rescue us from our difficult situations. He loves us and is greatly concerned about our needs. Peter tells us to "cast all our cares" upon Him, for He cares for us. (See 1 Pet 5:7) When the poor cry out, the book of Job describes the cries of the oppressed as capturing God's attention. "He hears the cries of the needy." (See Job 34:28 & James 4:5 NLT) The Lord promises not only to listen to the cries of the afflicted, but also to respond. He warns His people, "Do not take advantage of a widow or an orphan. If you do and they cry out to me, I will certainly hear their cry." (Ex 22:23) King David declared, "Is anyone crying for help? God is listening, ready to rescue you." (Ps. 34:17 MSG)

Somehow, many of us have embraced the idea that we need to have it all together before we can approach God in prayer. Instead, He encourages us to come to Him with our problems, pain, confusion, and doubts. In essence, He is saying, "Don't try to pretend you are ok when you're not. Be real!" David was honest with God as his prayers ran the gamut of emotions. On one occasion David prayed, "I'm caught in a maze and can't find my way out, blinded by tears of pain and frustration." (Ps. 88:8 MSG) When we approach God with the same transparency,

God is quick to respond. As it says in Psalm 51:17, "a broken and a contrite heart, O God, you will not despise."

The Lord invites us to come to Him when we are distressed. Jesus said, "Come to me, all you who are weary and burdened, and I will give you rest." (Matt:11:28) Jesus understands our predicament because He entered into a world cloaked in darkness and experienced the shame and brokenness that causes our pain. In His life and death, He bore our sorrows and grief.

An awareness of our human frailty is sharpened by crisis–a reality which is ever present but often forgotten when life is going well. The illusion of living a life independent from God is removed when calamity strikes. We are created to be dependent upon Him. In this sense, crises can be an opportunity. The quicker we shed the illusion of self-sufficiency, the sooner we open ourselves to receiving and giving more of His love. Our awareness of our need for the Lord will increase as we grow in relationship with Him.

When we pray, we show God that we trust Him to meet our needs, placing our lives in His hands. Paul exhorts us "not to be anxious about anything, but in everything, by prayer and petition, with thanksgiving, present your requests to God." (Phil 4:6) Prayer can eliminate anxiety! Joseph Scriven's hymn declares the needlessness of anxiety: "O what peace we often forfeit, O what needless pain we bear. All because we do not carry everything to God in prayer!" As we bring our need for help and guidance to the Lord, wonderful opportunities present themselves to experience His faithfulness, receive His wisdom and behold His power. In so doing, God is glorified!

Throughout the bible are recorded several testimonies of those who needed help and "called" or "cried" unto the Lord. As David testified, "I lift up my eyes to the hills — where does my help come from? My help comes from the LORD, the Maker of heaven and earth." (Ps 121:1-2) The Lord says, "Call upon me in the day of trouble; I will deliver you, and you will honor me." (Ps 50:15) The prophet Jonah also testified, "In my distress I called to the Lord, and he answered me." (Jonah 2:2)

While God cares deeply about our needs, He has something more profound to offer us in prayer. The essence of prayer is not a shopping list of things we need from God; it's God Himself. He is the heart and soul of prayer! He is always more important than anything we could ask for or imagine. The main purpose of prayer is to know Christ. The Lord's desire is that the cry of our hearts will be for Him, not just for what He can do. For many of us, once a crisis has resolved, our prayers stop. When needs are met, our pursuit of God ends. Even though needs come and go, Christ abides forever and He desires for us to abide with Him.

Without realizing it, prayer can become a religious duty required to remain in good standing with God. People can pray frequently and consistently with little or no feeling. Methods of prayer can become more important than content. If learned methods of prayer aren't followed it may seem as though true prayer hasn't taken place. To some, prayer can only happen in holy postures, such as folding your hands, bowing your head or getting on your knees. Others seem to think that God can only hear if they yell, cry, or speak in tongues. On the other end of the spectrum, silence before God may be emphasized. By which method does God hear us?

A variety of different forms, habits and styles of prayer are illustrated by the heroes of the bible. Jeremiah's posture was to stand before God when he prayed for God's people (Jer 18:20). Peter knelt to pray (Acts 9:40), while Nehemiah sat down as he prayed (Neh 1:4), Abraham prostrated himself (Gen 17:3), and David prayed on his bed (Ps 63:6). Ezekiel prayed in a loud voice (Ezek 11:13), Hannah prayed silently to the Lord (1 Sam 1:13), yet Paul prayed and sang in the spirit (1 Cor 14:15). David prayed in the morning (Ps. 5:3) however, Isaac prayed in his field during the evening (Gen 24:63). Daniel prayed in his house three times a day (Dan 6:10), while Anna prayed night and day in the temple (Luke 2:37).These practices are all good and we can learn from them. They reveal that the Lord does not judge a prayer based on the outward posture or the strength with which the words are spoken, but rather on the intent of the heart. The Lord spoke to the Prophet Samuel, "The LORD does not look at the things man looks at. Man looks at the outward appearance, but the LORD looks at the heart." (I Sam 16:7) Our relationship with God is far more dynamic than a mechanical form. We pray with our lives and not merely with our lips. The Lord longs for a heart to heart relationship in prayer.

Prayer is not meant to be a spiritual discipline in which

we strive to please God or work to make ourselves acceptable to Him. The good news is our Father longs to love us unconditionally and waits for us to come to Him! There's no need to climb a spiritual ladder in order to move closer to God. When tempted to do this we simply need to realize that God has come to us through the Lord Jesus Christ. God made Himself approachable by becoming a man. Through Jesus, the inaccessible was made accessible. Jesus is and always will be "Immanuel" God-with-us.

In that accessibility, God gave us the greatest gift we could ever receive. David understood this as he proclaimed, "The Lord is *my* Shepherd, I shall not be in want." (Ps 23:1 Emphasis added) And again when he said, "My health may fail, and my spirit may grow weak, but God remains the strength of my heart; *he is mine forever.*" (Ps 73:25-26 NLT Emphasis added). The focus of David's heart was God Himself. The Shulamite declared it this way, "I belong to my lover and *my lover is mine…*" (Song of Songs 6:3 Emphasis added) The Shulamite was proclaiming that she belonged exclusively to God and therefore could claim Him as her sole possession.

Jesus told the Samaritan woman at the well, "If you knew the *gift of God* and who it is that asks you for a drink, you would have asked him and he would have given you living water." (Jn 4:10 Emphasis added) Jesus said, "If you *knew* the *gift of God…* you would have *asked.*" This is an invitation. It requires a response. Jesus is the gift of God! See Him as the hidden treasure, the pearl of great price! There is no greater gift we can receive. The gift that God offers us in prayer is the opportunity to know Him and His heart. When we receive Jesus and encounter Him we are encountering God Himself. Instead of striving in prayer we can learn to receive in prayer. "Prayer," according to George A. Buttrick, "is friendship with God. Friendship is not formal, but is not formless: it has its cultivation, its behavior, its obligation, even its disciplines; and the casual mind kills it… Prayer is listening as well as speaking, receiving as well as asking; and its deepest mood is friendship held in reverence."[2]

Prayer is a choice to be with Jesus. Jesus said that Mary chose the "one thing" that is needed, and that hers was the better choice! (Lk 10:42) Despite the other pressing needs around her, Mary saw the incomparable riches in Christ. "The light of the knowledge of the glory of God in the face of Jesus Christ shone in her heart." (2 Cor 4:6 NKJV) Mary chose Jesus. She chose to be with Him. Mary came and sat at Jesus' feet. Prayer is so simple. Outwardly it's coming, sitting, and listening to God. It is also beholding Him and responding to His words. Inwardly it's loving, adoring, fellowshipping, and sharing life together.

Some have interpreted Mary's "one thing" to be merely a devotional time to read the written word of God and make our petitions for the day. This type of encounter is like reading a restaurant menu without ever eating the meal. Simply reading the word is vastly different than partaking of the living word. Jesus said, "The words I have spoken to you are spirit and they are life." (Jn 6:63) Prayer is coming to Jesus, sitting at His feet and being impacted by His Spirit and Life.

When Mary sat at Jesus' feet, she was clearly captivated. Her gaze was fixed on Him. When we pray, do our eyes rest upon the Lord with intense focus? Have you ever watched new parents gaze at their baby? Or the way a runner looks at the finish line as he nears the goal? The writer of the book of Hebrews exhorts us to "fix our eyes on Jesus, the author and perfecter of our faith, who for the joy set before him endured the cross, scorning its shame, and sat down at the right hand of the throne of God." (Heb 12:2) Hebrews encourages us to fix our eyes on the One who radically loves us and completely gives Himself to be with us. When our concept of prayer is coming to Jesus, the lover of our soul, sitting at His feet and listening to His voice; the exhortation to "fix our eyes on Jesus" becomes our delight. This should be the reason for prayer.

As the book of Hebrews notes, the Lord Jesus is the author of prayer. As the source and instigator of prayer, Jesus has the authority to define His role and ours. His desire is to relate to us as Father and Bridegroom. Likewise we are to relate to Him as sons, daughters and bride. By faith, we can enter into this relationship which He initiated and defined, and can grow into a place of wholeness and maturity.

Jesus conquered our sin and death not merely to set us free from the ultimate consequences of sin, but to remove the barrier that kept us separated from Him. The Victorious One is now exalted at the right hand of the throne of God. The cry of His heart is "Father, I want those you have given me to be with me where I am." (Jn 17:24) From the sacrificial love of Jesus, our relationship with Him was born. Prayer is the active expression of that relationship. Prayer is the dynamic means by which Jesus can fulfill His desire to love and commune with us. Christ the exalted One becomes the essence of prayer, the very heart of prayer and therefore He is the main attraction and focus of prayer. Jesus wants us to drink deeply of His love and to discover the reality of who He is, which is beautiful beyond human description.

When our hearts have been touched by the One who sacrificed His all for our love; sitting at His feet is not a burden or religious duty but a spiritual delight. What attracted Mary to the feet of Jesus was Jesus. She saw in the eyes of Jesus the love of God and it captured her heart.

A PRAYER FOR INTIMACY

O Beautiful Savior, I, so many times in the past, have been driven to my knees by the crises in my life. I pleaded with You to rescue me from my present situation; and if You did, I promised to serve You. How foolishly ignorant of me to think I could use my promise of service as a bargaining chip. You have no need of servants. You are looking for lovers who give their lives freely to you out of love. Heaven is not filled with indentured servants but with free sons and daughter who are lovers of You. You need nothing, but you desire my heart. You have loved me with an everlasting love, showing Your love through Jesus Christ.

Father I thank you that You are approachable in Jesus Christ. I am accepted by You just as I am. I don't have to climb a spiritual ladder to reach You. You, out of love, have come down to me in Jesus Christ. You are "Immanuel" God-with-me. Instead of striving in my prayer, help me to rest in You; help me to receive Your love.

Jesus, bound by Your own love, You have given yourself to me! It is not a burden to sit at your feet, but a delight. I come to sit, to listen, to receive and to respond to You.

Lord Jesus, You said, if I knew the *gift of God* I would ask and You would give me living water. Oh, Gift of God, I am asking: immerse me into this living water! Quench my inner thirst with Your living presence. I am asking You now for more of You.   Amen!

Chapter Six

The Father's Longing

"A Christian life rooted in the secret place where God meets and walks and talks with His own, grows into such a testimony of Divine power that men feel its influence and are touched by the warmth of its love. That, surely, is the purpose of all real prayer." E.M. Bounds

What is it that draws us to God? Why do some people respond to Jesus while others don't? Throughout the gospels, Jesus invited individuals to follow Him and fellowship with Him. For some, Jesus' message was difficult to accept. It challenged their culture, social structure and most of all their ambitions. Yet for others, His message struck such a deep chord that they whole-heartedly embraced it. When Jesus taught at the home of Martha, Mary, and Lazarus, three orphans, He revealed God's heart to them. The disciples and other guests who gathered there heard His message, but Mary responded to His words. She fearlessly and openly responded to Jesus by literally sitting at His feet and drinking in every word He spoke. (See Lk. 10:38-42)

Why was Mary drawn in such a way to Jesus? Though her thoughts are not revealed, her actions indicated that she realized she was in the presence of a safe, loving person who cared deeply for her. Mary was drawn toward the light of the Father's love shining through the face of Jesus. His love reflected the tenderness of a father to a daughter. Intuitively, Mary knew she could trust and believe in Jesus. This trust drew her to kneel at His feet. Jesus proclaimed, "I am the way and the truth and the life. No one comes to the Father except through me." (Jn 14:6) Sitting at the feet of Jesus is the same as approaching the throne of grace where the Father abides. The only work we are asked to do is "to believe in the one he (the Father) has sent." (Jn 6:29) As we sit at the feet of Jesus, we like Mary express faith in the revelation of our Father's love as revealed in the life of Jesus.

The Apostle John announced, "No one has ever seen God. But the one and only Son is himself God and is near to the Father's heart. He has revealed God to us." (Jn 1:18 NLT) Our English word, "revealed," is translated from a Greek word which means "to lead out." It portrays the idea of "bringing something out where it can be seen," "making known," or "unveiling." Jesus' incarnation brought out from behind the veil the affection and character of the invisible God. To a world full of orphans, Jesus revealed the creator and sustainer of the universe as Abba Father.

Mary grasped the idea that Jesus, who revealed the Father's heart, was God. She sensed that by drawing close to Him she was drawing close to God. Her Jewish upbringing may have caused her to form a completely different concept about God, but her spirit sensed the truth. Jesus was Her Lord, yet she knew she could approach the Father through Him. Our own prayer life can be dramatically changed by this revelation. It is essential for us to comprehend that the Father is just like Jesus and Jesus is just like the Father. The book of Hebrews points out that "He is the sole expression of the glory of God [the Light-being, the out-raying or radiance of the divine], and He is the perfect imprint and very image of [God's] nature..." (Heb 1:3 AMP) Jesus, in His humanity, is the perfect expression of the glory of God. He revealed what God is like. Paul strengthens this thought by declaring: "Christ is the visible image of the invisible God." (Col 1:15 NLT) He is the exact representation of the heart of God.

In Christ, God is reconciling the world to Himself, waiting with loving desire for us to come to Him. As Christians, we may believe this intellectually, but frequently there is a huge gap between what we believe and what we actually practice in prayer. Understanding and growing in intimacy with God can be a slow process. Jesus said to Philip, "Don't you know me, Philip even after I have been among you such a long time? Anyone who has seen me has seen the Father. How can you say, 'Show us the Father'? Don't you believe that I am in the Father, and that the Father is in me?'" (Jn 14:9-10) Like Phillip, it can take years to grasp what Jesus said about Himself. Preconceived ideas about God can block us from experiencing an intimate relationship with Him as Father. If God is seen as an austere judge who is unapproachable or if He is viewed as sentimental saying "Everything is all right" then our relationship with Him will be flawed. If we capture the fact that God is the embodiment of love and truth we will be lead into a genuine relationship with Him.

It is vital for us to allow Jesus, that is, His person, His life, His death, and His resurrection to shape our understanding of God. The revelation of "Christ crucified" shocks our natural senses and invalidates the ideas of God derived from human wisdom. A crucified Messiah was a stumbling block to the Jews because they were expecting a victorious Prince who would deliver them from the tyranny of the Romans. To the Gentiles, who sought after wisdom above all else, Christ's death was sheer madness. To their way of thinking, it was foolishness to believe that God would deliver His people by a man who could not deliver Himself. (See 1 Cor 1:22-25) Throughout history, many have struggled with the concept of Jesus' suffering and death by crucifixion. But Paul makes known that "God's weakness is stronger than the greatest of human strength." (1Cor 1:25 NLT) God revealed Himself as a suffering Messiah taking upon Himself the sins of the world because that is who He is. God doesn't pretend or act out of character. He is always Himself. The fact that God is willing to put Himself in a place of vulnerability is an amazing revelation regarding the depth of His love and desire to bring us into relationship with Him.

Our identity is based in part upon the relationships and roles we are given in life. To my wife, I am a husband. My daughter relates to me as her father. Through Jesus, we become sons and daughters of God who invites us to relate to Him as our Father. The life Jesus lived on earth demonstrated the relationship we can have with our heavenly Father. Our communion with Him, particularly our prayer life, is the expression of that relationship. Thankfully, Jesus taught us how to pray by His example and His words. The gospel of Luke describes the disciples as watching Jesus pray and they asked Him to teach them. "One day Jesus was praying in a certain place. When he finished, one of his disciples said to him, "Lord, teach us to pray, just as John taught his disciples." He said to them, "When you pray, say: 'Father'…" (Luke 11:1-2) When Jesus said "Father", He was not only telling us *what* to pray but also showed us *how* to relate to God in prayer. By beginning our prayers with "Abba Father," they take the form of a father/child conversation.

For Jesus to instruct His disciples to use the words "Abba" and "Father" when addressing God in prayer was probably shocking. These terms are so personal and familiar; it must have seemed disrespectful to approach the eternal, Almighty God in such a manner. The intimacy Jesus has with the Father makes this invitation possible. The Scripture records the affirming words of the Father to Jesus when He was baptized: "And as he was praying, heaven was opened and the Holy Spirit descended on him in bodily form like a dove. And a voice came from heaven: "You are my Son, whom I love; with you I am well pleased.'" (LK 3:22) Throughout His life, Jesus made reference to the depth of His relationship with His Father. He said: "I tell you the truth, the Son can do nothing by himself; he can do only what he sees his Father doing, because whatever the Father does the Son also does. For the Father loves the Son and shows him all he does." (Jn 5:19-20) Even while in the garden of Gethsemane as Jesus agonized over His coming crucifixion He continued to address God as Abba Father. He prayed, "Abba, Father, everything is possible for you. Take this cup from me. Yet not what I will, but what you will." (Mk 14:36)

Through our personal faith in Jesus Christ, we enter into a new identity as sons and daughters of God. Scripture reiterates this fact: "Yet to all who received him, to those who believed in his name, he gave the right to become children of God–children born not of natural descent, nor of human decision or a husband's will, but born of God." (Jn 1:12-13) Paul writes, "You are all sons of God through faith in Christ Jesus..." (Gal 3:26) and John declares, "Everyone who believes that Jesus is the Christ is born of God." (1 Jn 5:1) Becoming a child of God is a gift of the Father's grace.

As followers of Christ, the prayer of faith means constantly believing in the revelation of the Father's affectionate love. It is this faith, anchored in His love, which gives us confidence to "continue to work out (our) salvation with fear and trembling, for it is God who works in (us) to will and to act according to his good purpose." (Phil 2:12-13) Paul explains that this faith is "activated and energized and expressed and works through love." (AMP Gal 5:6)

The New Testament writers, particularly John, go to great lengths to emphasize the importance of understanding how much God the Father loves us and how we can openly approach Him. The apostle John enthusiastically proclaims, "How great is *the love the Father has lavished on us*, that we should be called children of God! And that is what we are! The reason the world does not know us is that it did not know him. Dear friends, now we are children of God..." (1 John 3:1-2 Emphasis added) A composite of John's words from various translations might read something like this: "Behold, gaze upon, stare at, and meditate on what incredible, awe-inspiring, marvelously wonderful, and astonishingly great love the Father has lavishly bestowed on us!"

Just as the Apostle John was awestruck by the revelation of God's love, we too may reflect in awe on the incredible love the Lord has lavished on us. John stressed the fact that we are "now" the children of God. Grasping this concept has the potential to change our fundamental identity and our prayer life. Our prayers are expressions of who we think we are before God.

How do we become awestruck with God's incredible love? How can we embrace it? God provided the way through His Holy Spirit who enables us to speak from the depths of our heart the words: "Abba, Father." "*The Spirit himself testifies with our spirit that we are God's children.* Now if we are children, then we are heirs — heirs of God and co-heirs with Christ..." (Rom 8:15-17 Emphasis added) The Holy Spirit bears witness with our spirit that we are God's sons and daughters. The Father touches our spirit with His Spirit and we become consciously aware that we are loved and affirmed as His children. Because of this confirmation by the Holy Spirit, we become sensitive to the fact that we are tremendously valued by the Father. We are valuable not because of what we do, but because of who we are in Him. This frees us to come to Him in prayer out of pleasure and delight, rather than out of a sense of duty or an effort to earn His favor.

Once we grasp in our heart and in our spirit who we are to God, we can come boldly to the throne of grace without fear of rejection. We do not have to approach the Lord as if He were an unconcerned ruler requiring a prescribed ceremonial form of address. We can come directly to Him as Abba Father. Christ has revealed that God is a loving, tender, caring father who desires and delights in being approached and embraced by His children. He delights in our desire to spend time with Him for He desires to spend time with us. Listen to the prophet Zephaniah: "For the Lord your God is living among you. He is a mighty savior. He will take delight in you with gladness. With his love, he will calm all your fears. He will rejoice over you with joyful songs." (Zeph 3:17 NLT) The Father is so delighted that He sings joyfully over us with exuberant songs. You may wonder how He can rejoice over us despite our failures and weakness. His word tells us in response: "Love... bears all things, believes all things, hopes all things, and endures all things." (I Cor 13:7 NKJV) Love can bear, believe, hope, and endure because love perceives everything through different eyes. Love knows things we do not know. Love has the power to create the beauty of holiness where there is none. The Father has loved us with an everlasting love. (See Jer 31:3) His heart is fully engaged in drawing us into the circle of His love.

A more profound truth of the Father's love is that He loves us with the same measure and intensity as He loves Jesus, His only begotten Son. Listen to this request Jesus made to His Father: "May they be brought to complete unity to let the world know that you sent me and *have loved them even as you have loved me.*" (John 17:20-23 Emphasis added) The Father not only loves us, but He loves us with the same magnitude that He loves Jesus. What a stunning, life changing revelation!

J. I. Packer said, "God receives us as sons, and loves us with the same steadfast affection with which He eternally loves His beloved only begotten. There are no distinctions of affection in the divine family. We are all loved just as fully as Jesus is loved… This, and nothing less than this, is what adoption means. No wonder John cries, "Behold, what manner of love!" When once you understand adoption, your heart will cry the same."[1]

When we believe this truth by asking for the affirmation of the Father's love in our heart and experience His love through the infilling of His Spirit, our faith and confidence in Him will continually soar. Embracing the love of the Father is where we will find our rest, our security, and our peace, allowing us to live and operate out of this place of awesome love. This is what Paul prayed for: "And I pray that you, being rooted and established in love…" (Eph 3:17) Once our hearts are rooted in the rich soil of the Father's love, the foundation to build our lives upon is established and unshakeable. Prayer then becomes a way of life, rather than an obligation. Prayer becomes more about growing in relationship and friendship with our Father.

At the age of nine, my five siblings and I were placed in an orphanage. Since a family of six children was difficult to place in one home, we were divided. After living in the orphanage for a year, my sister and I were placed with one family, while the other four were put with another family. The father of our new home was a kind person who wanted me to call him "dad." In my mind, it was too soon for me to use such an intimate term with a man I barely knew. I lived in his house, ate his food, and wore the clothes he bought for me, but I couldn't enter into a father/son relationship with him. In fact, I never called him dad. At the time of our placement into this family, my biological parents were still alive, but unfit to parent. Despite this fact, I still dreamed about my family being united again. This dream was a major obstacle preventing me from developing a new father/son relationship. The emotional attachment I had for my old family prevented me from bonding with this new "father." Even though he offered to be my dad, I felt like a distant outsider, not a son, so I couldn't share my thoughts or dreams with him. As a result, we were unable to connect as father and son. Our relationship deteriorated and by the end of one year, my sister and I were taken back to the orphanage.

In less than a year, another family welcomed us into their home. By this time I was 11 years old and was beginning to realize the impossibility of my original family being restored. The father of this home was different from all the others I had encountered. His love and acceptance of me seemed genuine. I felt I could trust him. One thing he did from the beginning that greatly impacted me was to introduce me as his son. He never said, "This is Cliff, my adopted son." He said, "This is my son." Slowly, I began to call him dad. At first it was awkward but in time became easier and then natural. Although I was not consciously aware of it, a shift was taking place in my heart and in my life; this person became my dad! I loved spending time with him. He took me fishing, hunting, and camping. I enjoyed sharing my thoughts and my dreams with him. He would listen, then affectionately share the wisdom and values that governed his life. Through his actions and words, he taught me the importance of loyalty and friendship, as well as how to relate to people on a day to day basis.

Something even deeper and more significant took place after I was adopted. As an orphan, I felt rejected, abandoned, even unwanted. But in this new family, I was wanted. They chose me. I was chosen by two people who wanted me to be their son, who desired to love me as a part of their family. They were not rich; they actually struggled financially at times because they had taken my sister and me into their home. Their sacrificial love greatly impacted my heart. I am forever grateful that my adoptive parents found me, opened their hearts to me and blessed me with a much better life than I would have had growing up in my original home or the orphanage. Feeling accepted and loved,

I began to reap the benefits of a healthy father/son relationship for the first time in my life. This relationship healed several emotional wounds and saved me from many more as I went through my teenage years.

God has extended an invitation to each of us to join His family. Now it is our turn to respond. When we accept Jesus Christ as our Lord, we receive the love of the Father as His adopted children. Forgiveness of sins and justification are fantastic blessings, but we are more than forgiven sinners or pardoned criminals. We become part of the family of God. Accepting our heavenly Father's invitation will open the door to experience the fullness of His love. It requires an act of faith, a step of trust in His unconditional love. As we rest in the fact that our acceptance is not based on our performance but in our Father's love, trust will develop. He knows that the only way we will trust Him is to personally experience His goodness (See Ps. 34:8) Faith and trust in His acceptance leads to an even greater encounter of His goodness and experience of His affectionate love. This is the principle revealed by the Apostle John when he stated: "We love Him because He first loved us." (I John 4:10) It is vital to understand that the experiential love of the Father is the foundation of our lives; the soil in which the roots of our life draw nourishment. Just as I needed to take a step toward accepting the love of my earthly adoptive father, we also need to open our hearts to the unconditional love and affection of our heavenly Father.

In the face of Jesus, Mary met the Father her heart had

longed for all her life. Sitting at His feet, Mary basked in the radiant warmth of the Father's love. She was safe. Her heart was quieted within her. She was at rest. Father God had become Abba to her. She took that vital step in drawing near to Christ. If she had remained at a distance, watching from the kitchen, what would she have missed? When we take that step to sit at Jesus' feet, we too will see Abba in the face of Jesus and experience His love. Abba will become our exceeding great reward and prayer will become communion in the secret place of our heart.

A PRAYER FOR INTIMACY

Lord Jesus, You are in the Father, and the Father is in You. You spoke the words of Your Father and did the miraculous works of Your Father who dwells in You. (Jn 14:10-11) Lord Jesus, You stated that You are the way and the truth and the life. No one comes to the Father except through You. (Jn 14:6) I believe that You are the way to the Father, the truth about the Father and have the life of the Father. You showed me the Father. You revealed that the Father longs to be Abba to me; that Abba is Holy Love and desires me to be close to Him. Every time I come to you Father, I feel as though I've come home. I am at rest. My desire is to bask in the radiant warmth of your love and acceptance. May Your Spirit touch my spirit whereby I can freely cry, from the depth of my heart, "Abba Father." I don't want to live at a distance. I intend to live out my life each and every day before You and with You as Your beloved child. Abba, You are the gracious Father in whom my heart has always longed for. Father, You have caused my heart to be at peace in Your presence. I ask for the Spirit of wisdom and revelation so that I am able to know You more intimately. You are the melody of my heart; You make my heart sing. Being with You overwhelms me with pleasure; there is no other place in this world I would rather be. I will enter Your gates with thanksgiving and your courts with praise for I am entering into the presence of the One who loves me and enjoys me.

Amen!

Chapter Seven

Living Confidently With Abba

"O eternal Mercy, you who cover over your creatures' faults! ... O unspeakable mercy! ... My heart is engulfed with the thought of you! For wherever I turn my thoughts I find nothing but mercy! ... O immeasurably tender love! Who would not be set afire with such love!"

Catherine of Siena

Approaching the Father in prayer as a beloved son or daughter is a step of faith. The Apostle Paul instructs us to be "rooted and grounded in the love of God." (Eph 3:17) When we choose to believe that we are indeed God's sons and daughters, we are planting ourselves in the rich soil of the Father's unfailing love. Prayer is the pursuit of knowing God's heart and seeking a relationship with the Father through the Son by the Holy Spirit. When we are established in the Father's love, the language of prayer will cease to be a performance and be transformed into vibrant fellowship. As we experience the graciousness of the Father's heart toward us, we in turn become more transparent with Him and begin to live out true fellowship with God.

Our desire to be with God and our ability to be real with Him in prayer are made possible by the Father's unconditional love. It is the key that unlocks the door to intimacy with Him. If we are unable to believe in His unconditional love; we have no basis to be confident before Him in our failure and brokenness. Most children know they can be truthful with their parents when they make mistakes or break the rules. Children may be upset or anxious about the possible consequences of their actions, but usually don't fear losing the love of their parents or being shamed by them. Likewise, if we cannot picture the true expression of the Father's face when we sin, we will stand ashamed before Him, praying out of fear and doubt. Inevitably, we will adopt a self-centered, self-protective posture in prayer; trying to appease God by hiding behind religious expression rather than being truthful. This protective posture will cause our hearts to remain at a comfortable distance from Him. Admittedly, the thought of living openly and honestly before God can be daunting! We all come short of God's glory on a daily basis, and it is easy to become consumed by shame and guilt rather than to receive God's love, acceptance and forgiveness. Isaiah points out that the sinners in Zion were gripped with fear and asked this question: "Who of us can dwell with the consuming fire? Who of us can dwell with everlasting burning?" (Is 33:14) From their perspective, a fiery God must be kept at a distance; approaching too close to Him would surely consume them. Likewise we may fear drawing close to a Holy God will cause us to be overcome with guilt and shame. His presence, which is actually the most merciful, loving place we can turn to, might feel unsafe. Succumbing to shame and guilt causes us to shrink back rather than draw near to Him.

In order to confidently approach the Father, we must have a picture of His love to help us take those first steps. The biblical parables provide a great place to start. The parable that perhaps best reveals the Father's heart is "The Prodigal Son." This parable might have been more accurately titled "The Prodigal Father," because it reveals the extravagant love and acceptance of God the Father toward His children. The word "prodigal" means "reckless, extravagant, lavish, and superabundant;" in this story, it describes the unsurpassable grace the Father pours out on His repentant sons and daughters. In reading this parable, we uncover wonderful clues revealing God's perspective towards us as we come to Him in prayer. The parable begins with the son's story:

> "There was a man who had two sons. The younger one said to his father, 'Father, give me my share of the estate.' So he divided his property between them. Not long after that, the younger son got together all he had, set off for a distant country and there squandered his wealth in wild living. After he had spent everything, there was a severe famine in that whole country, and he began to be in need. So he went and hired himself out to a citizen of that country, who

> sent him to his fields to feed pigs. He longed to fill his stomach with the pods that the pigs were eating, but no one gave him anything. "When he came to his senses, he said, 'How many of my father's hired men have food to spare, and here I am starving to death! I will set out and go back to my father and say to him: Father, I have sinned against heaven and against you. I am no longer worthy to be called your son; make me like one of your hired men.' So he got up and went to his father." (LK 15:11-20)

When the prodigal son "came to his senses," he had an important revelation; he realized that he would be better off in his father's house as a servant. He had observed his father treating hired servants with respect and wondered if perhaps he could earn his father's respect again by working for him. On the son's long journey home, he probably berated himself with a torrent of critical thoughts. I can imagine his rant: "I blew it as a son and took my father for granted. I was so caught up in my own desires that I wished my father dead so I could have my inheritance. He will never accept me back as his son. Maybe, my father will show kindness by letting me work as a hired man. At least I would be better off than I am now." Although he may have been correct to acknowledge and regret his poor choices, the son was greatly mistaken regarding his father's character. Like many of us, the prodigal son did not know his father's heart towards him. He had a partial, distorted impression of who his father was. In his mind, his father's forgiveness, acceptance and love was something he would be required to earn. His logic might be summarized as, "I am no longer worthy to be called your son so I must work as a servant to earn your approval." What he soon discovered was that his father's love was not something to be earned but rather a gift to be received.

The story shifts to reveal the perspective of the father:

> "But while he was still a long way off, his father saw him and was filled with compassion for him; he ran to his son, threw his arms around him and kissed him. The son said to him, 'Father, I have sinned against heaven and against you. I am no longer worthy to be called your son.' "But the father said to his servants, 'Quick! Bring the best robe and put it on him. Put a ring on his finger and sandals on his feet. Bring the fattened calf and kill it. Let's have a feast and celebrate. For this son of mine was dead and is alive again; he was lost and is found.' So they began to celebrate." (Lk 15:20-24)

At first glance, the father's response to his son is not at all what one might anticipate. In our minds, this father who had been abandoned and dishonored, surely had the right to give his son a verbal lashing or at the very least, to express heartfelt disappointment regarding the son's choices. We would expect him to be more cautious about receiving his wayward son. Shouldn't the father immediately establish boundaries and conditions if his son was to remain on the premises? We may also wonder why the father doesn't seem more offended by his son's disrespect and distance himself from him. Shouldn't the son have been placed on probation until he could demonstrate he was a changed man?

On the contrary, it is apparent by the father's actions that he was not angry. He does not shame or chastise his son. Instead, while still at a distance, he ran to embrace his son. He literally could not wait for him to arrive and rushed out to meet him. Bear in mind that culturally, a father was a greatly respected figure in those days. Furthermore, men of nobility never ran and such behavior was socially unacceptable. But this father not only ran, he smothered his son in an embrace before the son could request forgiveness. The Greek implies that the father "covered him with kisses." This father was so overcome with love that he cast aside dignity and protocol to welcome his repentant child. His uncontainable joy in his son's homecoming is a picture of how God receives us when we return to Him. Love eclipses all other concerns.

What do we expect when we come to God in prayer? Many of us are like the prodigal son in that we expect an angry God who is disappointed because of our sins. When we sin, we are often less likely to run to the One who longs to forgive us. Instead, old habits, vices or unhealthy relationships may appear more safe and comfortable. More positive choices may be made by seeking comfort in jobs, church or social activities, but nevertheless, God is kept at a distance. At best our comforts provide temporary relief. At worst, they leave us in a place of denial and distance from God. Sadly, when we eventually turn to God, we may feel it is necessary to earn His love by saying the right words or being on our best behavior.

When struggling with sin is combined with the concept of an angry God, despair is often the end result. At times, we may think God is merely tolerating us, growing tired of our struggles, and losing patience with our weaknesses. If we believe God is upset with us our hearts will remain guarded. With a guarded heart, sin will produce shame, fear, and guilt, rather than quickly leading to repentance, forgiveness and a transformed heart. Shame, fear and guilt are powerful forces that can keep us from going deeper in our relationship with the Father. But if we embrace the revelation of the Father's heart as revealed in the story of the prodigal son, we will realize that His love is unlike any love we have ever experienced. Our Father's thoughts about us are radically different from our thoughts and His ways are drastically different from our ways. (See Isaiah 55:8-9)

Every morning, God the Father is waiting for you with a heart of compassion and delight matching that of the prodigal son's father. He is overjoyed when you come to Him in prayer and runs out to embrace you, no matter what you may have done or said the day before. God's love is like this on a daily basis. He never stops loving you and me! This parable is not a snap shot of the Father's love when we're first saved, but an ongoing movie of what His heart is like all the time! God's love does not change. (Mal 3:6) He loves us because He is love and that is who He is. When we approach Him in brokenness and repentance, He will embrace us with His kisses of forgiveness. We do not deserve nor can we earn His love. His love is not for sale, if it were, it would cease to be love. That's the beauty of the Father's unconditional love. Our challenge is to embrace, not run from His extravagant, affectionate love.

The parable of the Prodigal Son is also a reflection of reconciliation. In this parable, the father's heart reveals what God has disclosed about Himself in the Scriptures. Throughout history God has offered forgiveness of sins and a desire to be reconciled to His people. In His word, God reiterates over and over again that His forgiveness is total and complete. How can this be possible? It is possible because Christ took our place and paid our penalty! John the Apostle points out that: "He loved us and sent his Son as a sacrifice to clear away our sins and the damage they've done to our relationship with God." (I Jn 4:10 MSG) Therefore, "If we confess our sins, he is faithful and just and will forgive us our sins and purify us from all unrighteousness. (1 Jn 1:9)

If you were to trek north toward the North Pole, and continue on without changing direction, you would eventually be going south. However, it is not true when you go east or west. Heading west and continuing in the same direction will cause you to continually go west. The East will never be reached. In a sense, the east is an infinite distance from the west. The Psalmist spoke of this phenomenon when he stated, "as far as the east is from the west, so far has he removed our transgressions from us." (Ps 103:12) In saying this, God has declared that our sins have been removed an infinite distance from us. Through Christ's atoning sacrifice, God can freely forgive our sins and effectively clear away the damage they have caused to our relationship with Him.

Isaiah the prophet declared "You have loved back my life from the pit of corruption and nothingness, for You have cast all my sins behind Your back." (Isa 38:17 AMP) Casting something behind ones back puts it out of sight and out of the way. This is what God has done with our sins. They are invisible to Him and no longer an obstacle between Him and us. When sin is removed, we have new life. The father of the prodigal son said, "For this son of mine was dead and is alive again." (Lk 15:34) So it is with us; God loves us back to life through His forgiveness and acceptance. Paul proclaimed, *"because of his great love for us, God, who is rich in mercy,* made us alive with Christ even when we were dead in transgressions — it is by grace you have been saved." (Eph 2:4-6 Emphasis added) The Lord's forgiveness is total and complete. Our sins can no longer impede the restoration of our fellowship with Him.

The Bible goes to great lengths to describe God's mercy. The prophets indicate that God is not only merciful but also delights in showing mercy. Micah, one of the prophets, offers yet another picture when he proclaimed, "Who is a God like you, who pardons sin and forgives the transgression of the remnant of his inheritance? You do not stay angry forever but delight to show mercy. You will again have compassion on us; you will tread our sins underfoot and hurl all our iniquities into the depths of the sea." (Mic 7:18-19) Our sins are not dropped into shallow water where they can be easily retrieved. Instead, God purposefully hurled them into the depths of the sea where they cannot be found. He did this because He delights in showing mercy. Who do you know that "delights" in showing mercy? Most often, in our lives, mercy is a gift given in a begrudging manner. However, the image of the prodigal son's father running to and embracing his son illustrates that our God and Father delights in mercy. God really is the "blessed God and Father of our Lord Jesus Christ, the Father of mercies and God of all Comfort." (2 Cor 1:3)

Not only does God delight in showing mercy, but when He forgives our sins, He truly forgets them. The Lord speaks through the prophet Isaiah declaring, "I, even I, am he who blots out your sins." When we repent, our sins are removed from the record, never to be remembered again. No longer remembering our sins is a promise to never bring them up again. "Love keeps no record of wrongs." (1 Cor 13:5)

The prodigal son's acceptance back into his family was not based on his confession or good behavior, but solely on the father's mercy and forgiveness. In much the same way, God's forgiveness enables us to freely return to Him. The Lord declares through Isaiah saying, "I have swept away your sins like a cloud. I have scattered your offenses like the morning mist. Oh, return to me, for I have paid the price to set you free." (Isa 44:22 NLT) He Himself paid the price to set us free; paving the way for our return to Him.

Repentance is a process by which we are drawn into the loving embrace of a forgiving and accepting Father. It is His love that causes us to repent. Paul exhorts us never to "underestimate the wealth of His kindness and forbearance and long-suffering patience." (Rom 2:4) He reminds us of the all-important truth that it is God's kindness which leads mankind to repentance. Repentance in part means to change one's mind, accepting God's will rather than our own. Thus it is God's loving-kindness, not His judgment that leads us to repent. The Bible encourages us to "fearlessly and confidently and boldly draw near to the throne of grace (the throne of God's unmerited favor to us sinners), that we may receive mercy [for our failures] and find grace ... for every need [appropriate help and well-timed help, coming just when we need it]." (Heb 4:16 AMP)

Once we truly believe the Father loves us unconditionally and wholly embraces us as He did Jesus; His love creates an environment of joyful freedom in our heart. Mercy has a way of dissipating our fear, shame, and guilt. "There is no fear in love. But perfect love drives out fear, because fear has to do with punishment. The one who fears is not made perfect in love." (1 Jn 4:18) Paul said, "Anyone who trusts in him will never be put to shame." (Rom 10:11) When we go to the Father, He removes the shame placed upon us by our sins. The Psalmist declared, "Those who look to him (the Father) for help will be radiant with joy; no shadow of shame will darken their faces."

(Ps 34:5 NLT) The Father promises that if we look to Him for mercy, not even a shadow of shame will cross our faces; we will be radiant with joy. Consequently there is no need to cover up our weakness or faults since we know He loves us. His response will always be merciful and gracious.

As recipients of God's mercy, we in turn begin to experience a new and greater love for the Lord. David cried out, "I love the Lord, for he heard my voice; he heard my cry for mercy. Because he turned his ear to me, I will call on him as long as I live." (Ps 116:1-2) David's heart was impacted by the Lord's mercy, creating in him a passionate love for God and a life-long commitment to call on His name. When a heart is impacted by extravagant mercy it causes that heart to be influenced by that mercy. Mercy received produces a loving heart.

Another example of an individual responding to mercy is found in Luke chapter 7. While Jesus was eating dinner in the home of Simon, a Pharisee, a woman whom the Bible describes as immoral, heard He was there and brought a beautiful alabaster jar filled with expensive perfume. She knelt before Him, at His feet, weeping. Her tears fell upon His feet and she wiped them off with her hair. She kept kissing His feet and rubbed them with the expensive perfume. When the Pharisee observed this, he remarked to himself, "If this man were a prophet, he would know what kind of woman is touching him. She's a sinner!" Jesus responded to Simon by telling him a story:

> "A man loaned money to two people—500 pieces of silver to one and 50 pieces to the other.

> But neither of them could repay him, so he kindly forgave them both, canceling their debts. Who do you suppose loved him more after that?" Simon answered, "I suppose the one for whom he canceled the larger debt." "That's right," Jesus said. Then he turned to the woman and said to Simon, "Look at this woman kneeling here. When I entered your home, you didn't offer me water to wash the dust from my feet, but she has washed them with her tears and wiped them with her hair. You didn't greet me with a kiss, but from the time I first came in, she has not stopped kissing my feet. You neglected the courtesy of olive oil to anoint my head, but she has anointed my feet with rare perfume. "I tell you, her sins—and they are many—have been forgiven, so she has shown me much love. But a person who is forgiven little shows only little love." (Luke 7:36-47 NLT)

God's extravagant mercy washed over this woman, removing her sins and causing her heart to burst with abundant love. Her love for Him was poured out in tears of joy and kisses of affection. She humbly knelt before Him, displaying her gratitude with a costly sacrifice of fragrant perfume. Mercy received creates a heart overflowing with love. Jesus remarked that the woman loved much because she was forgiven much. He also commented: "But a person who is forgiven little shows only little love." Is Jesus saying that those who have lived a horrible sinful lifestyle will love Him more than those who haven't? Most assuredly not! He is merely pointing out that those who know the cost of their sins and recognize the depth of love that paid for their sins will love more than those who don't understand this.

When we ponder sin, we generally think about it in terms of how it impacts others or us. Even from that perspective we minimize in our mind the damage our sins cause. As David considered his sin with Bathsheba, he revealed God's perspective when he cried out to God and confessed his sin: "Have mercy on me, O God, according to your unfailing love; according to your great compassion blot out my transgressions. Wash away all my iniquity and cleanse me from my sin. For I know my transgressions, and my sin is always before me. Against you, you only, have I sinned and done what is evil in your sight, so that you are proved right when you speak and justified when you judge." (Ps 51:1-4) David's confession shows that committing sin against another person is breaking God's law, thus sinning against God. David reveals here that all sin is primarily an offense against a loving and holy God.

Often sin is categorized into degrees of severity, based on how offensive it may seem and how it affects others. Most of us would rate those who rape, kill or steal as the worst sinners. However, the Bible tells a different story, stating the greatest sinner is one who breaks the greatest commandment, which is "to love God with all our heart, with all our soul, with all our mind, and with all our strength." (Matt 22:37) Neglecting to love God with our whole heart is sinning against Him. There are many consequences to sin, but the one we frequently fail to notice is: sin brings pain to God. When God is spurned we forget that our rebellion hurts Him. People are hurt to the degree that they have loved, and God has loved us more than anyone. Paul asked, "Are you [so blind as to] trifle with… and underestimate the wealth of His kindness and forbearance and *long-suffering patience?* Are you …actually ignorant [of the fact] that God's kindness is intended to lead you to repent…?" (Rom 2:4 AMP Emphasis added) Long-suffering indicates that God suffers long in the patience of love.

The prodigal son's sin was primarily against his father. His interest lay more in his inheritance than in his relationship with his father. As he fostered this attitude in his heart, ingratitude eventually turned into indifference and ultimately into rejection. The father was rejected by his son. In spite of this offense, the father showed great mercy. So it is with our heavenly Father. When we realize God is merciful, a gift that can not be earned through our good works and good words, we will surrender our hearts to the Father's tender love. Through prayer, we can receive God's mercy and forgiveness, obtaining His love and acceptance as beloved children. In so doing, we can, like the prodigal son, restore and renew our relationship with Him.

The ending of the prodigal son parable illustrates the father embracing his son and immediately ordering his servants to bring the best robe, ring, and a pair of sandals to place upon him. These items are symbols of sonship. The prodigal son was welcomed back as a son, not as a servant. Ps 103:10 states, "He does not treat us as our sins deserve or repay us according to our iniquities." God welcomes us back as His sons and daughters.

As we learn to relate to the Father as sons and daughters, guilt, shame and fear of rejection will no longer hold us captive. This freedom allows us to respond naturally and spontaneously from our heart. New believers can go to the Father with child-like faith without fearing rejection for their immaturity. Other believers who struggle in sin can confidently approach God, knowing He will show mercy and forgive their sins, giving grace to overcome them. God's love allows us to be completely transparent before Him without religious airs or rituals. His love liberates us from performance-based prayer and gives us the freedom and security to be real while exposing our deepest feelings to Him. We can speak to Him in words that reflect our heart. Like King David, we can invite Him to: "Search me, O God, and know my heart; test me and know my anxious thoughts. See if there is any offensive way in me, and lead me in the way everlasting." (Ps 129:23-24) Only by receiving His tender love into the deepest chambers of our heart will we be able to banish fear and embrace true intimacy.

When we know we are loved and accepted by Abba it births an incredible expression of love in our heart for Him. Suddenly we can respond to Abba with our whole personality. This covers the entire range of our human emotions and reactions. When we come before the Lord in this manner, we may at times find ourselves laughing and singing while at other times, crying and weeping. Prayer also involves listening to the voice of Abba; waiting, reflecting, and meditating on what He shares. As we reflect, there may be times of sorrow, confession, and repentance.

When Abba speaks or shows us Himself through His word, surrendering, yielding, submitting, and obeying is often involved. As our spirit yields and draws close to God, abiding in Him, clinging to His words, and beholding Him in worship are all experienced in the environment of God's unconditional love and acceptance. This communion happens in the context of loving fellowship with "the Father of mercies and God of all Comfort." (2 Cor 1:3) As you can see, prayer has all the dynamics of a genuine relationship.

When we come to Abba Father in prayer, it is important to see Him eagerly waiting by the roadside of our day looking down the path for signs of our coming. As He catches sight of us, He runs to us with loving compassion on His face. Abba meets us with His compassionate embrace kissing us again and again with the kisses of His forgiveness, unconditional love and acceptance. This is the picture of our Father, who is eagerly anticipating our arrival each time we come to Him. Prayer is the place where the reality of heaven can touch earth and a heart on earth can touch heaven.

A PRAYER FOR INTIMACY

Abba Father, I am amazed by Your mercy. When I sinned against You and offended You personally, I did not expect nor did I believe that You would be waiting eagerly for me to return to You. I was expecting an angry God pointing His finger and hurling accusations, but instead You embraced me bestowing Your kisses of forgiveness upon me. Though I came to you guilty, deserving punishment, planning to work my way back into Your good graces; You would have nothing of it. You loved my life back from the pit of corruption and nothingness, casting my sins behind You. Your love keeps no record of my wrongs. Your compassion never fails. Open the floodgates of heaven and pour out Your love, for you are love! Father, show me the depths of Your love! Your mercies are new every morning; great is Your faithfulness.

Amen!

Chapter Eight

Listening To Abba

"I always begin my prayer in silence, for it is in the silence of the heart that God speaks. God is the friend of silence- we need to listen to God because it's not what we say but what He says to us and through us that matters."

Mother Teresa

The most important element of prayer is listening. Hearing our Father's voice is the secret to having assurance and confidence that He will listen to us.

We are invited to pray because God the Father first spoke to us. The Father is the initiator of prayer and we are the responders. As our Father, God gives us, his children, life-sustaining words which enable us to draw close to Him. As Jesus declared, "Man does not live on bread alone, but on every word that comes from the mouth of God." (Matt 4:4) When God's words penetrate our hearts, our lives inevitably change.

Listening attentively comes naturally when we pursue our passions. Our favorite music draws our attention because we love the feelings evoked by its melodies, rhythms and words. As we listen closely to the Father speak, our hearts are stirred with delight. As with wonderful music, God's words may energize us or help us to find rest or they may inspire and ignite feelings of love and connection within us. The word of God is meant to create a living dialogue in our hearts with God Himself. His words reflect His heart and in turn our hearts are touched. We are awed by the sense that God is speaking to us and intensely loves us. How can we help but respond? The bible conveys that God is moved when we respond to Him with genuine love. The Psalmist conveys God's response by saying: "A broken and a contrite heart, O God, you will not despise." (Ps 51:17) Praying from the heart, where our deepest and sincerest feelings reside, moves us closer to Him.

Mary of Bethany loved God deeply and hungered for more of His love. Ignoring the social protocol of her day, she "sat at the Lord's feet listening to what He said." (Luke 10:39) In a room filled with tension, Mary was able to listen attentively because of her love for God. She not only heard the word with her ears; she also listened attentively with her heart. When we love someone deeply, we focus intently on their words, drinking them in eagerly. Mary, who was a lover of God, listened as a lover. How do you and I listen? As servants? As employees? As students? What is our posture when we listen to God? Do we find ourselves distracted or doubtful? Or, are we attentive, resting in the confidence that the words we hear are spoken in love? Jesus warned His disciples, "Therefore consider carefully *how* you listen." (Lk 8:18 Emphasis added) It is essential to hear the word of God with the ears of a lover, feeding on the revelation of His love because He is the source and life of love. "We love because he first loved us." (1 Jn 4:19)

God chose an interesting way to speak to me regarding heartfelt listening. At a time when I was seeking to grow in intimacy with the Lord, I asked God to show me a book of the Bible to pray through as I read. Immediately, the Holy Spirit placed the book of Proverbs on my heart. At first I was surprised by this. My desire was to pray through a book of the bible that focused on God, not man. The book of Proverbs primarily deals with relationships on a horizontal level rather than on a relationship with God. I wanted to continue to develop a deeper bond with the Lord and could not imagine how Proverbs would help!

As I pondered this, the Holy Spirit spoke to my heart: "If you pray the book of Proverbs, I will show you My heart and reveal My thoughts to you." With that word of encouragement I began to daily read Proverbs chapters one through ten. By verse 23 in chapter one, God had captured my attention. "If you had responded to my rebuke (listened to my counsel), I would have poured out my heart to you and made my thoughts known to you." Now, I was excited about pursuing the Lord in Proverbs! After reading a week of Proverbs, the Holy Spirit asked me this question: "Who wrote Proverbs?", "King Solomon." I replied. He asked me another question: "To whom did he write it?" "To the citizens of His kingdom," I said, thinking these were very basic questions. To my surprise, I received a small rebuke. "Read it again!" the Holy Spirit instructed me. So, I read chapter one through ten again. Then I saw it. King Solomon was not writing to his subjects; he wrote as a father to his sons. The phrase "my son" is mentioned 22 times in the book. Here are just a few examples:

> "Listen, my son, to your father's instruction and do not forsake your mother's teaching." (Prov 1:8)
>
> "Listen, my sons, to a father's instruction; pay attention and gain understanding." (Prov 4:1)
>
> "Listen, my son, accept what I say, and the years of your life will be many." (Prov 4:10)
>
> "My son, pay attention to what I say; listen closely to my words." (Prov 4:20)

The book of Proverbs is a training manual on wise living written by a father to his sons. Solomon told his sons that his father, King David, taught him wisdom. "When I was a boy in my father's house, still tender, and an only child of my mother, he taught me and said, 'Lay hold of my words with all your heart; keep my commands and you will live. Get wisdom, get understanding; do not forget my words or swerve from them.'" (Prov 4:3-5) The main purpose of Proverbs is to give instruction to a son or daughter in order that they may "get wisdom" and be successful to reign in life. Solomon taught his son that "By me (wisdom) kings reign and rulers make laws that are just; by me princes govern, and all nobles rule on earth." (Prov 8:15) Every Father wants their son to grow into a position where they are able to take responsibility and represent him well.

Our Heavenly Father wants to train His sons and daughters with His wisdom so that we too can "reign" in this life through Christ Jesus. He encourages us to ask for wisdom when we lack it, promising to provide it generously. (James 1:1-5) Paul encourages us "to keep asking the God of our Lord Jesus Christ, the glorious Father, to give us the Spirit of wisdom and revelation, so that we may know him better." (Eph 1:17) Notice the primary reason for the Spirit of wisdom and revelation is to know the Father better.

What is wisdom and how can we receive it? Wisdom is to understand the heart of God and walk in the light of that understanding. We receive wisdom by living in close relationship with the Father, listening to and hearing His voice, then choose to live by His words. This involves leaning on, clinging to, relying on, and trusting in the Father's words. The ability to listen is one of the most important elements of a wise heart. A good example of a wise man that did not develop the skill of heeding wisdom is King Solomon. I have often wondered how "the wisest man" became foolish in his old age. The answer is found in King Solomon's own words when he requested wisdom. Solomon asks the Lord in 1 Kings 3:9, to "give to your servant an understanding heart to judge your people that I may discern between good and evil." (NKJV) The word "understanding" in the Hebrew is the word "sama" which means "to hear, to obey, to listen." One of the well known uses of this word is found in Deut. 6:4 "Hear, O Israel, The Lord our God, the Lord is one." One way to translate 1 Kings 3:9 is "give your servant a listening heart so that I may possess discernment." The source of wisdom did not come from Solomon. As he stopped listening to the Lord and relied more upon himself, he became a fool. It can be tempting to rely upon the knowledge and experience we accumulate throughout the years rather than upon the Lord Himself. The word "listen" is mentioned 17 times in Proverbs. Here are some additional examples.

> "My son, *pay attention* to my wisdom, *listen well* to my words of insight,…" (Prov 5:1 Emphasis added)

> "Now then, my sons, *listen* to me; pay *attention* to what I say." (Prov 7:24 Emphasis added)

> "Now then, my sons, *listen* to me; blessed are those who keep my ways. Listen to my instruction and be wise; *do not ignore* it." (Prov 8:32-33 Emphasis added)

> "*Listen*, my son, and be wise, and keep your heart on the right path." (Prov 23:19 Emphasis added)

> "Blessed is the man who *listens* to me (wisdom), *watching* daily at my doors, *waiting* at my doorway." (Prov 8:34 Emphasis added)

King Solomon essentially tells his sons that wisdom is obtained through listening. (Prov 23:19). When King Solomon stopped listening to the Lord and relied upon his own understanding, he violated the revelation he had received regarding wisdom. He lost sight of his credo: "Trust in the Lord with all your heart and lean not on your own understanding; in all your ways acknowledge him, and he will make your paths straight." (Prov 3:5-6) King Solomon had received a wealth of understanding throughout his life but in the end, he stopped trusting the Lord which resulted in leaning on his own knowledge.

As I continued reading Proverbs during my devotionals, I sensed the Holy Spirit encouraging me to read it as a son. Realizing that a son's perspective should help me hear my Father from a different point of view, I eagerly continued on my journey. Approximately one week into this adventure, I grew frustrated having not received any new insights. I came to the realization that I actually did not know how to listen and receive as a son should from his father. "How does a *son* listen to his father?" I wondered. "How *do* I connect to my heavenly Father the way a son connects to his earthly father?" "Where can I go to learn how to listen like a son?" Turning to the gospels to see how Jesus listened and related to His Father seemed to be a logical place to start. As I read, I came across the following passage:

> "At that time Jesus prayed this prayer: 'O Father, Lord of heaven and earth, thank you for hiding these things from those who think themselves wise and clever, and for revealing them to the childlike. Yes, Father, it pleased you to do it this way!'" (Matt 11:25-26 NLT)

Jesus praises His Father for hiding His wisdom from the so-called "wise" and revealing it to those who are "childlike". While praying Jesus stated that those who are like a child will receive the revelation of the Father. What does childlike mean? A young child is innocent, pure, trusting, and views life in an uncomplicated simple manner. God unfolds the riches of His wisdom to those who are pure in heart and able to trust Him completely.

Reading on in this passage, an interesting statement is made by Jesus. "My Father has entrusted everything to me. No one truly knows the Son except the Father, and no one truly knows the Father except the Son and those to whom the Son chooses to reveal him." (Matt 11:27 NLT) The Greek word for "truly knows" can be translated as "to have a full and experiential knowledge of." Apparently, what Jesus is telling us in this passage is that He alone has a complete, experiential knowledge of the Father. This verse also affirms that it is Christ and Christ alone who reveals that knowledge. The Father has entrusted everything to Jesus, who states He will reveal the Father to whom He chooses. How does Jesus choose to whom He will reveal the Father? The answer is in the following verse.

> "Then Jesus said, 'Come to me, all of you who are weary and carry heavy burdens, and I will give you rest. Take my yoke upon you. Let me teach you, because I am humble and gentle at heart, and you will find rest for your souls. For my yoke is easy to bear, and the burden I give you is light.'" (Matt 11:28-30 NLT)

Notice the order of the words spoken by Jesus: "Come to Me", "take my yoke", and "let me teach you". Those who will learn to listen and receive from the Father as a son or daughter are the ones who draw close to Jesus and take His yoke. Taking His yoke comes before learning. We can understand some things about God before taking Jesus' yoke; but will not obtain experiential knowledge of the Father until after receiving the yoke He offers.

Going to Jesus and placing His yoke upon us, positions us to learn from Him. What is the yoke of Christ? Some have described it as a gentle and humble heart, but this definition seems incomplete and inaccurate. Gentleness and a humble heart are indeed character traits we will learn when yoked to Jesus, but they are not the yoke itself. The yoke has also been portrayed as a symbol for submission to Christ's specific interpretation of the law. This is partly true, for in fact the yoke is a symbol of submission. Examples of this can be found in ancient literature. For instance, when a person submitted to a particular rabbi's teaching, he was considered to be yoked to that rabbi. Therefore when we accept Jesus' teaching we are submitting to Him. But Jesus offers much more than just His teaching when we become yoked to Him. How does Jesus' yoke differ from a rabbi's yoke?" The primary difference is that the yoke Jesus offers is born out of a relationship between the Father and the Son, whereas a rabbi's yoke is strictly academic.

As we take Jesus' yoke upon ourselves, we become attached to the Son who provides an avenue for us to learn to be sons and daughters to our heavenly Father. It is through Jesus alone that we have access to the Father. (see Jn 14:6) And it is only Jesus who can truly reveal the full, experiential knowledge of the Father to us. (See Matt 11:27) Jesus described His yoke as "easy to bear" indicating it is not a master/slave relationship which can be harsh and cruel. Instead, He is offering a loving relationship built on a close father/ son bond. Because the Lord is gentle and humble, His yoke is easy and good. The Message Bible translates Matthew 11:29-30 this way: "Walk with me and work with me — watch how I do it. Learn the unforced rhythms of grace. I won't lay anything heavy or ill-fitting on you. Keep company with me and you'll learn to live freely and lightly."

The dynamic connection between the Father and the Son is displayed in the gospels as they retell how Jesus walked and worked with the Father. Jesus knew He was the Father's beloved Son. Their relationship was rooted and established in love. The Father publicly proclaimed that Jesus was His beloved Son in Matt. 3:17: "And a voice from heaven said, "This is my Son, whom I love; with him I am well pleased."

It was from this position of unconditional love that Jesus lived His life, accomplished His work, and gave Himself for the sins of the world. The assurance of the Father's unconditional love, allowed Jesus to walk in humility, remain in a place of rest and from that place listen to His Father. Jesus said, "The world must learn that I love the Father and that I do exactly what my Father has commanded me." (Jn 14:31) The following Scriptures reveal the heart of Jesus as a son yoked by love to His Father.

> "*By myself I can do nothing*; I judge *only as I hear,* and my judgment is just, for I seek not to please myself but him who sent me." (Jn 5:30 Emphasis added)

> "I tell you the truth, the Son *can do nothing* by himself; he can *do only what he sees* his Father doing, because *whatever the Father does* the Son also does. For the Father loves the Son and shows him all he does." (Jn 5:19-20 Emphasis added)

> When you have lifted up the Son of Man, then you will know that I am [the one I claim to be] and that *I do nothing on my own* but speak just what the Father has *taught me*." (Jn 8:28 Emphasis added)

Jesus humbled Himself before the Father, surrendering His will completely to Him. He said He "can do only what he sees his father doing." He only "speaks just what the Father has taught Him." Jesus had an incredible relationship with His Father. He voluntarily put Himself in total submission to Him. Jesus, the Eternal Son, who became man, lived His entire life in total dependency on His Father. Everything Jesus said or did came out of this relationship of love. He did not view Himself as being alone or functioning independently, but rather as eternally connected to His Father. Jesus said, "The one who sent me is with me; he has not left me alone, for I always do what pleases him." (Jn 8:29) Surrendering oneself out of love is the dynamic of true fellowship; this is the heart of prayer.

When we come to Christ and take His yoke, we can rest confidently in the fact that we are now "in Christ." Being in Christ we are loved, accepted, and embraced as sons and daughters by God the Father. The book of Hebrews reveals that "Jesus and the ones he makes holy have the same Father. That is why Jesus is not ashamed to call them his brothers and sisters. For he said to God, 'I will proclaim your name to my brothers and sisters.'" (NLT Heb. 2:11-12)

It is important to understand that God desires to speak to each and every one of us as His beloved sons and daughters. The bible reveals that the Father "decided in advance to adopt us into his own family by bringing us to himself through Jesus Christ. This is what he wanted to do, and it gave him great pleasure." (Eph. 1:5 NLT) Because God is a father, He longs to speak *personally* to each one of us just as our earthly parents do. He also desires that we listen to His words of life and wisdom. King Solomon told his son, "My son, pay attention to my wisdom, listen well to my words of insight." (Prov 5:1) The Father does not just speak to an elite few who may have successful ministries, but equally to all His children. The question is "Are we listening?"

The ability to listen can be hindered when we cease to abide in Christ. Jesus taught His disciples to "Abide in Me, and I in you. As the branch cannot bear fruit of itself, unless it abides in the vine, neither can you, unless you abide in Me. I am the vine, you are the branches. He who abides in Me, and I in him, bears much fruit; for without Me you can do nothing." (Jn 15:4-5 NKJV) Again He reiterates in verse 7: "If you abide in Me, and

My words abide in you, you will ask what you desire, and it shall be done for you." In Verse 9 Jesus adds: "As the Father loved Me, I also have loved you; abide in My love." Jesus modeled this type of relationship with His Father, living His life in total dependency on the Father and drawing His life source from the Father. This same truth is spoken of by Peter in 2 Peter 1:3-4: "His divine power has given us everything we need for life and godliness *through our knowledge of him* who called us by his own glory and goodness. Through these he has given us his very great and precious promises, so that through them you may participate in the divine nature and escape the corruption in the world caused by evil desires." (2 Pet 1:3-4 Emphasis added) Everything we need for life and godliness is in Jesus. We receive His divine power and life through continual fellowship with Him.

The word "abide" has been translated in other translations as "remain, remain united, dwell, live," and as "make your home." Jesus said, if we do not dwell, live, or remain in Him and His word does not dwell, live, or remain in us then we cannot be fruitful. Jesus teaches that it is essential to remain united with Him for without Him we can do nothing. Part of abiding in Christ and His love has to do with continually living in the truth of our new identity as beloved sons and daughters. "Continually" means it is our place of permanent residence. Where we live affects *how* we live. As we begin to reside in the Father's love, we will have an increased desire to listen closely to Him. We will eagerly anticipate our time to talk with Him and hear His words. We will ache to be at His feet on a daily basis. We will also hunger and thirst for His word. Our hearts will agree with Job and Jeremiah. Job declared, "I have treasured the words of his mouth more than my daily bread." (Job 23:12) Jeremiah testified, "When I discovered your words, I devoured them. They are my joy and my heart's delight…" (Jer 15:16 NLT) "Delight" means to "enjoy, to love, to take pleasure in" and "to value something highly." King David expressed His delight and love for the word of God throughout Psalm 119. It appears that every word from God to David was like a divine kiss to David's heart.

> "I rejoice in following your statutes as one rejoices in great riches. I meditate on your precepts and consider your ways. I delight in your decrees; I will not neglect your word." (Ps 119:14-16)
>
> "Your statutes are my delight; they are my counselors." (Ps 119:24)
>
> "For I delight in your commands because I love them. I lift up my hands to your commands, which I love, and I meditate on your decrees." (Ps 119:47-48)
>
> "If your law had not been my delight, I would have perished in my affliction." (Ps 119:92)
> "Oh, how I love your law! I meditate on it all day long." (Ps 119:97)
>
> "How sweet are your words to my taste, sweeter than honey to my mouth!" (Ps 119:103)
>
> "Your statutes are my heritage forever; they are the joy of my heart." (Ps 119:111)

> "Trouble and distress have come upon me, but your commands are my delight." (Ps 119:143)
>
> "I rejoice in your promise like one who finds great spoil." (Ps 119:162)
>
> "I obey your statutes, for I love them greatly." (Ps 119:167)

David was not indifferent to God's word. On the contrary, his heart was emotionally charged by it. The word brought joy and pleasure to his heart. It was sweeter than honey to his mouth. Abba desires to have sons and daughters who enjoy His word, not simply those who follow it. Imagine treasuring His words more than daily food. If we see the intent of God's heart, then our hearts will grasp His words with delight and everything He speaks will be like a divine kiss.

We have a daily invitation to enter into His glorious presence of love and mercy. Solomon proclaimed, "Blessed is the man who listens to me [wisdom], watching daily at my doors, waiting at my doorway." (Prov 8:34) As we take deliberate steps every day to spend time waiting and listening for our heavenly Father to speak, anticipate that He *will* speak. God encourages us to come with expectation by giving to us His promises. Through Jeremiah the prophet, God encourages us to call to Him and promises to answer: "Call to me and I will answer you and tell you great and unsearchable things you do not know." (Jer 33:3) As we come daily in dependence upon Him, the Father "wakens us morning by morning, wakens our ear to listen like one being taught." (Isa 50:4)

Since the Lord prompted me to read Proverbs through the eyes of a son, I have noticed a heart-felt response rising up from within. When I read phrases containing "my son" or "listen, my son," I respond to the Father by saying "Father, speak! Your son is listening." Or, "Father, I hear Your voice in this passage." Those phrases remind me that my heavenly Father is personally speaking to me. The Father is not an absentee Father but one who waits for us each morning to "waken" the ears of our heart to be taught by Him.

Jesus instructs us: "When you pray, go away by yourself, shut the door behind you, and pray to your Father in private. Then your Father, who sees everything, will reward you." (Matt 6:6) This private, secret place is where Jesus developed intimacy with His Father. Like Jesus, we need to find a place away from the crowds and distractions of life. Entering into the secret place allows us to quiet our hearts enabling us to hear Abba's still small voice. Henri Nouwen succinctly describes the purpose of solitude this way: "Solitude and silence are for prayer. The Desert Fathers did not think of solitude as being alone, but as being alone with God. They did not think of silence as not speaking, but as listening to God. Solitude and silence are the context within which prayer is practiced."[1]

"Be still, and know that I am God." (Ps 46:10)

As I consider my personal journey of discovering intimacy

with Abba, I am overwhelmed with emotion by the depth of His love. Each day, His expression of love for me continues to grow deeper and richer. His love is a never ending story!

A PRAYER FOR INTIMACY

Father, I want to abide in Your love. One thing I desire and that is to make my heart at home in Your amazing love. Your love adopted me into Your family. Daily, help me to embrace the truth that I am Your beloved child. Abba, give me ears to hear Your voice and receive Your wisdom as a son. You provided the Holy Spirit who imparts wisdom, revelation and life. Like Mary, I want to be one who sits at Your feet patiently waiting and attentively listening for You to speak. Abba, awaken my heart morning by morning so I can hear Your voice. Your voice kindles a fire of Holy passion within my heart. Father, You are the center of my world; the object of my affection. I am listening! Come Abba, speak to my heart. Amen!

NOTES

Chapter Two

1. C.S. Lewis, The Great Divorce (A Touchstone Book) P 46

2. Roxanne Brandt, Ministering To The Lord (Whitaker House) pg 19

3. A.W. Tozer, The Knowledge of The Holy (Harper & Row) p.39

4. Henri J.M. Houwen,The Only Necessary Thing
(A Crossroad Book) P.79 Quoted from Henri's book
"Compassion: The Core of Spiritual Leadership -- A crossroad Book,
The crossroad Publishing Company New York copyright © 1999
by The Estate of Heri J.M. Houwen

Chapter Three

1. A.W. Tozer, The Knowledge of the Holy (Harper & Row) P 9

2. J. Rodman Williams, Renewal Theology Vol 1
(Academie Books) P 51-52

3. Julian of Norwich, quote in "The book of Jesus"
Edited by Calvin Miller Pub Simon & Schuster P 197
Copyright 1996

4. Devern Fromke, The Ultimate Intention (Sure Foundation) p 56

Chapter Four

1. Augustine was a theologian and a major Christian writer that lived in the fourth century AD.

NOTES

2. Catherine of Siena, Little Talks With God (Paraclete Press) p 42 & 46

3. Catherine of Siena, Little Talks With God (Paraclete Press) p 35

4. Major Ian Thomas was quoted in the book "The book of Jesus," Edited by Calvin Miller p. 239

5. Psalm 144:3

CHAPTER FIVE

1, Clement of Alexandria (c. 345-407) Early church writer and philosopher John Knox (1515-1572) Leader of the Scottish reformation

2. George Buttrick (1892-1980) Anglo-American pastor and devotional writer

CHAPTER SIX

1. J.I. Packer, Knowing God (Downers Grove, IL. InterVaristy Press, 1973), P 196

2. Bernard of Clairvaux, The Love of God (Multnomah Press 1983) P 93

CHAPTER EIGHT

1. Henri Nouwen, The Way Of The Heart (Haper SanFrancisco) P 69

For additional copies of this book
or to contact Cliff Baker:

Mighty In Spirit Ministries
P.O Box 893
Rathdrum, ID 83858

or

mightyinspiritmin@gmail.com